More praise for T

"*The Whole Five Feet* is as eloquer... is a singularly gifted reader, and he deftly illustrates how books can save one's life."
—Helen Schulman

"Beha learns that the best literature doesn't shield us from the world but pushes us back out into it, albeit with fresh eyes. As he grapples with the death of his beloved aunt, a debilitating bout with Lyme disease, and other major and minor calamities, Beha finds that writers as diverse as Wordsworth, Pascal, Kant, and Mill had been there before, and that the results of their struggles to find meaning in life could inform his own. . . . In the end, Beha comes away with a deeper appreciation for literature's power to guide us through life than he ever got during his formal education."
—*The Seattle Times*

"Christopher Beha has written a unique memoir: intimate, confiding, deeply moving, and yet wonderfully informative and 'intellectual' in the very best sense of the word. Undertaking to read 'The Whole Five Feet' of classics of western civilization at a time of crisis in his personal life is an illuminating experience both for Mr. Beha and for the reader."
—Joyce Carol Oates

"'In much wisdom is much grief,' counsels the book of Ecclesiastes, and in Christopher R. Beha's tender intellectual memoir [of reading the Harvard Classics], we find plenty of both. . . . Life intruded rudely on Beha's sabbatical, and he rose to the occasion by writing an unexpected narrative that deftly reconciles lofty thoughts and earthy pain. In doing so, he makes an elegant case for literature as an everyday companion no less valuable than the iPod."
—*The New York Times Book Review*

"An original and highly addictive cocktail of bookshelf genres—family memoir meets extreme armchair adventure meets cultural criticism meets history of American education. To say this is an important book (and it is) is possibly to undersell its overriding virtue—that it is a sheer blast to read." —Heidi Julavits

"*The Whole Five Feet* is no book report; Beha's reflections are far the richer because he delicately wheels and dives among both the great writers' ideas and his own life experiences—proving, if we needed proof, of the greatness and centrality of reading. About John Stuart Mill, Beha reflects on the nature of pleasure and happiness, observing through the prism of his own illnesses, 'Your comfort, especially your physical comfort, isn't under your control, so you'd better find something else to work at.' The idea here is mature far beyond his years, and yet the style is all salt spray and blue sky."
—*Free Range Librarian*

"In *The Whole Five Feet,* Christopher Beha reads the classics of our inherited culture through the lens of his own life and reconsiders the canon—everything from Homer to Thoreau, Cicero to Cervantes—by groping for the humanity he has in common with these masters of the past. This book is exhilarating in its tenderness, its disabused calm, its acceptance of big tragedies and little comedies. I was profoundly moved by Beha's unexpected intertwining of erudition and lived life and grateful to spend several exalting evenings in his company." —Edmund White

Cambridge, May 1, 1909

I have undertaken to select from the best literature of the world a five-foot shelf of books to be published by P. F. Collier & Son under the title of "The Harvard Classics." The selection is intended exclusively for English-speaking people. As a rule, only complete works will be included in the series.

In making choice among the different works of a great author the aim will be to take the author's most characteristic work or that one which will be most intelligible to the people of to-day, or that which has proved to be the most influential.

Each separate work will be preceded by a concise introduction; and notes and glossaries will be provided whenever they seem likely to increase the reader's enjoyment and profit.

It is my belief that the faithful and considerate reading of these books, with such rereadings and memorizings as individual taste may prescribe, will give any man the essentials of a liberal education, even if he can devote to them but fifteen minutes a day.

Charles W. Eliot

The Whole Five Feet

The Whole Five Feet

What the Great Books Taught Me About Life, Death, and Pretty Much Everything Else

Christopher R. Beha

Grove Press
New York

Published simultaneously in Canada
Printed in the United States of America

ISBN-13: 978-0-8021-4485-0

Grove Press
an imprint of Grove/Atlantic, Inc.
841 Broadway
New York, NY 10003

Distributed by Publishers Group West

www.groveatlantic.com

10 11 12   10 9 8 7 6 5 4 3 2 1

For Mimi
and
For Paul and Michael

Contents

CONTENTS

Man is but a reed, the most feeble thing in nature,
but he is a thinking reed.

—Blaise Pascal

THE HARVARD CLASSICS

Charles W. Eliot

Introduction, or
"A Careful and Persistent Reader"

Volume L: Introduction; Reader's Guide; Indexes

A few moments before midnight on New Year's eve, while December 2006 prepared to pass into January 2007, I sat alone in the library of my parents' apartment on York Avenue in Manhattan. Twenty blocks uptown my mother and father, my brother and sister, my brother-in-law, and my cousins had gathered for a small party hosted by my aunt Mimi. Roughly the same distance downtown, though farther west, a million people stood shivering in Times Square. Halfway between my family and the rest of the world, I read the first pages of Benjamin Franklin's *Autobiography*.

In truth, I didn't feel much like celebrating.

A week earlier, on Christmas night, I'd suffered what television has taught me to call an "anxiety attack." That is, I'd sat up in bed, unable to sleep, my heart pounding so insistently that I thought I might choke on it. I got up and went into the library. (This scene, too, takes place in my parents' apartment.) I pulled a few books from the shelf, which is what I do when I'm feeling restless. But I couldn't read. I couldn't even see the words in front of me. Even if I could have seen them, I wouldn't have been able to concentrate enough to make sense of them. One by one I took the books down, opened and closed them, and then returned them to their place, the whole process like some compulsive tic.

After an hour of this, I woke my parents—something I'd done often in childhood but learned to stop many years ago. Weary but indulgent, my father followed me back to the library. I took up the same space on the couch where I'd sat for the past hour, and he flopped down in a chair across from me.

"What's the story?" he asked.

I considered the many ways I might answer this question.

"Don't know," I answered. "I can't sleep."

I don't remember precisely what we discussed from there, but I'm fairly sure that the subtext of our conversation was exactly what the hell I was doing waking him up in the middle of the night after a long Christmas dinner. My father is the kind of man to whom almost everyone he knows comes at one time or another for advice. He's unfailingly generous with his time and attention. But he holds himself—and, by some unspoken extension, the rest of us—to a standard. There is something about him that occasionally makes one feel the need to account for oneself. So I tried to explain.

This attack, such as it was, had been unprecedented but not wholly unexpected. At any rate, its causes weren't obscure to me. I was twenty-seven years old and in the process of moving back home. I'd spent the previous five years of my life writing a novel that no one seemed much interested in publishing. While doing so, I'd acquired several thousand dollars in credit card debt—debt that I was in no great danger of paying off any time soon, since I'd just quit my job. It was a good job: the hours manageable; the people friendly; the work, on balance, interesting. I'd told my boss (a family friend with whom I got along very well) that I was quitting because my writing was "taking off."

In fact, it was doing no such thing. But the truth was that she'd left me no choice: she'd promoted me and given me a raise. In fairness to her, it wasn't much of a promotion, nor much of a raise. Still, it was enough to make me feel a life I didn't want solidifying around me—a life in which I worked nine to five each day, came home to sleep for a few hours, and then sat up writing through most of the night; a life in which I felt tired every moment spent awake and restless every moment that I slept.

In addition to all this, I'd recently broken up with a girl I still loved, for reasons uncertain to me even at the time I did it. As I sat with my father in the library on Christmas night, the reasons for this breakup seemed to disappear entirely. That one compulsive and irreversible act stood in my mind for countless mistakes and broken promises.

Of course, as a necessary condition of our post-belated age, one can never merely feel adrift or turned against oneself. One must also hold certain awkward feelings about these feelings. One must recognize such malaise as banal and used-up, as a kind of American consumer indulgence. One must stand detached even from one's sense of detachment, alienated from one's own alienation. And so I dutifully did.

Some parts of all this I explained in a roundabout way to my father that night, though I left out the last bit entirely. (My dad isn't quite of a generation that never discusses its feelings, but he is of a generation that never discusses its feelings about its feelings.) After a few hours, I let him go back to sleep. Eventually I even managed to sleep myself. But our conversation continued in my head, on and off, throughout the week that followed, which I spent suffused with a vague but pervasive sense of ill-being. The feeling still lingered as I opened Franklin's book on New Year's eve.

I should say here that my odd choice of reading material wasn't arbitrary. *The Autobiography of Benjamin Franklin* is the first book in the first volume of the Harvard Classics—a fifty-volume set of "great books" compiled and published a century ago. Known informally as the Five-Foot Shelf, the set spans the time from the ancient Greeks to the end of the nineteenth century, and it includes poetry and fiction, history and philosophy, science and theology. Some months before that night in the library, I had decided to read the entire Shelf over the course of the year to come. It was then that I'd set this midnight appointment.

Why had I wanted to read these books in this way? Even now I'm not entirely sure of the answer to this question. Two sets of the Classics populated my childhood. The first belonged to my father. I can't remember ever seeing it taken down from the shelf, except during some dusting or reorganization, only to be quickly returned. Nor was its fate unique among the books in my childhood home. Not that my family didn't read—quite the opposite, in fact. But in addition to being a reader, my father is also a bibliophile (which is, of course, not the same thing) and an amateur book collector. It was in these latter capacities that he came somewhere along the way to own the Five-Foot Shelf—just as he came to own the collected papers of James Buchanan, an early edition of Tocqueville's *Democracy in America*, and any number of other books that lived out unattended existences in various corners of the house, far away from the well-thumbed novels, biographies, memoirs, and works of popular history and science that were in heavy rotation within the family.

The second set belonged to my maternal grandmother. Like the first, it had gone mostly untouched so far as I knew, but it had a much greater impact on me. My grandmother too was a reader, but she wasn't a collector of books as such, and that row of red cloth spines stood out starkly against the mixed colors of faded dust covers and trade paperbacks on her shelves. When she died—I was seven at the time—her house on the East End of Long Island became a family vacation home, and I often went to those shelves on rainy summer afternoons. The bulk of my grandmother's books were works of Catholic theology and of famous Catholic novelists like Greene and Waugh and Chesterton. There were also mysteries by Agatha Christie and my older cousins' schoolbooks. I spent some time on most of these, but I always came eventually to that long row of red.

Some of the titles I knew from a very young age: *Grimm's Fairy Tales; The Thousand and One Nights*. I had a vague grip on some of the others, in the odd-angled way that young children hold on to so much of the world. (I associated *The Voyage of the Beagle* with Snoopy.) But most of the titles were so foreign that they suggested nothing at all to me: *Plutarch's Lives; Letters and Treatises of Cicero and Pliny; On the Sublime*. Finally I would come to the very last volume, oddly labeled "Introduction." This always seemed—as it seems now—the best place start.

The introduction is written by Charles William Eliot, the man who edited the Harvard Classics. Eliot served as president of Harvard for four decades, from a few years after the end of the Civil War to a few years before the beginning of World War I. During that time, he transformed Harvard into the first modern American university and therefore the model for what a modern university should be. He changed undergraduate education through his experiments with elective courses and written exams while dramatically raising the standards of the professional schools. (His effort to bring written exams to the medical school was initially resisted on the grounds that many of its students were illiterate.) In the process of this work, Eliot also made himself one of the most prominent public figures in late-nineteenth-century America.

Throughout his tenure at Harvard, Eliot had occasionally remarked that "a five-foot shelf would hold books enough to give in the course of years a good substitute for a liberal education." As Eliot neared retirement in 1909, the publisher P. F. Collier & Son invited him to compile this Five-Foot Shelf. With the help of various professors at Harvard, he did so, and over the next two decades Collier sold almost half a million sets, representing tens of millions of individual volumes.

Unlike similar efforts, such as the Encyclopaedia Britannica's Great Books of the Western World, which have been updated and revised over the years, the Harvard Classics were fixed once for all. They are not an evolving project, but a picture of intellectual history as seen from Eliot's point of view in the first decade of the twentieth century. And it's in his introduction to the set that Eliot best explains this point of view.

I understood much of this introduction from an early age, at least in the most literal terms. Eliot has a straightforward style, and he makes his intentions clear from the very first sentence: "My purpose in selecting the Harvard Classics was to provide the literary materials from which a careful and persistent reader might gain a fair view of the progress of man observing, recording, inventing, and imagining from the earliest historical times to the close of the nineteenth century."

Eliot compiled the Harvard Classics not as a "great books" collection but as a course—several courses, really—of study. He hoped "to present so ample and characteristic a record of the stream of the world's thought that the observant reader's mind shall be enriched, refined and fertilized by it." In this spirit, the final two volumes include, in addition to his introduction, a set of lectures, an exhaustive index, and a reader's guide that breaks the contents down both by theme (The History of Civilization; Religion and Philosophy; Education; Science; Politics; Voyages and Travels; and Criticism of Literature and the Fine Arts) and by genre (Drama; Biography and Letters; Essays; and Narrative Poetry and Prose Fiction). With these tools in hand, Eliot's Five-Foot Shelf may be viewed as nothing less than the world's greatest textbook.

In the years after I first took it down from my grandmother's shelf, I returned to this one volume with some frequency. The Harvard Classics—the idea of them as well as their physical presence in this house—fascinated me. They appealed to me most immediately for the reason that similar projects appeal to so many people: they suggested the existence of a discrete and relatively stable canon, one that I might eventually conquer.

As my own literary ambitions developed, I came to believe that an exhaustive knowledge of literary culture was a necessary part of realizing them. The pursuit of knowledge was largely a pleasure, but it was nonetheless undertaken self-consciously, and it threatened occasionally to overwhelm me. In desperate moments, when I felt as though every book I read pointed to five others previously unknown to me for which I didn't have time, I told myself that I would one day read the Five-Foot Shelf, front to back, and be done with it. At school, when I read Cervantes, I was acutely aware that Sterne and Fielding still lay in wait. But over the summer I could go to that Shelf and check off *Don Quixote*, knowing that no other title could crop up in its place.

Given the (perhaps cheap) satisfaction this checklist approach
gave me, one might think I made some headway through the
list over those summers. But the point was always that the Shelf
would be there when I was ready for it. In the meantime, I rarely
got beyond the introductory volume. Eliot's introduction is the
shortest work in the series, the only one that can be read in a
sitting before turning on the afternoon baseball game. After the
nineteenth or twentieth time through, in fact, it can be read
during the baseball game.

One might conclude from my failure to get beyond it that I
wasn't yet one of Eliot's "careful and persistent" readers, that I
was more enamored with the idea of great books than with great
books themselves. But I'd like to think that there was more at
work. In fact, I was reading several books a week at this time in
my life (I am talking now about my last years of high school and
my first years of college). I just wasn't reading the kinds of books
that Eliot had chosen for his Shelf. Instead, I was reading the kind
of books I wanted to write, which is to say mostly novels. (To
be more precise: novels written by Americans in the second half
of the twentieth century; novels that set out explicitly to "subvert" the literary history represented by the Shelf; novels that
implicitly suggested that the "great books" were insufficient to
the particulars of the modern age.)

There is very little prose fiction in the Classics. "Literature,"
for Eliot, meant something different from what it typically
means now, when it's shelved at the opposite end of the bookstore from Philosophy, Religion, or History. This fact accounts
for much of why Eliot's project as a whole interested me, but
also for why I had not taken the logical next step of reading those
books. The Five-Foot Shelf, or at least Eliot's introduction to it,
depicts a cultural landscape that is almost entirely literary, a land-

scape in which books—more specifically, "works of literature"—
are the primary means of understanding and relating to the
workings of the world.

Like all great works, the Harvard Classics invent their own
audience, and this audience was still one I wanted to join. "I proposed to make such a selection as any intellectually ambitious
American family might use to advantage," Eliot explains, "even
if their earliest opportunities of education had been scanty."

Later, he elaborates:

> I hope that many readers who are obliged to give eight or ten
> hours a day to the labors through which they earn their liveli-
> hood will use the Harvard Classics, and particularly young
> men and women whose early education was cut short, and
> who must therefore reach the standing of a cultivated man
> or woman through the pleasurable devotion of a few minutes
> a day through many years to the reading of good literature.

Eliot's goal was fundamentally democratic. When the Classics appeared in 1909, 13 percent of the adult population had
finished high school, and only 3 percent had finished college. But
in Eliot's view anyone with fifteen minutes to spare at the end
of the day could acquire in a few years the best of what higher
education had to offer. Nonetheless, if a project like Eliot's were
undertaken now, it would have to be accompanied by an elaborate apologia. It would need to defend its existence from the dual
charges of irrelevance and elitism. Or maybe it would argue the
virtues of the "right kind" of irrelevance or elitism. But Eliot
doesn't worry about such charges. He takes for granted the
benefits of "cultivation." He has no doubt that there are a significant number of "intellectually ambitious" people who aspire

to this cultivation as an end in itself, and that such an end is best reached by "pleasurable devotion of a few minutes a day" to great literature.

There is much competition these days for those last twilit fifteen minutes. But Eliot was serenely confident not just that what he had to offer was valuable but that it would be recognized as such. Like the popular kid at school, Eliot appealed to me precisely because he trusted in his own appeal. Conversely, a crisis of confidence—a neurosis of the margins that can mask itself as arrogance—is a large part of what makes many contemporary defenders of the canon so unattractive.

The Harvard Classics were compiled not to stand out from their age or against a popular culture that undervalued their contents. Rather, they were a reflection of their age and its values. Eliot felt little need to argue the worth of these books, or of the "cultivation" they might provide, which he took to be self-evident. Nor was he offering membership in an exclusive club or a means of separating oneself from the common consumer of mass culture. He hoped to make a shared cultural birthright universally accessible. I wanted to be one of Eliot's industrious autodidacts, though in truth I was anything but self-taught. (Somehow, I managed to get as far as college and a few years of graduate school while still thinking of myself as fundamentally lacking in formal education.) Reading Eliot—and idly dreaming of reading further in the Classics—gave me not a feeling of superiority but a sense that my interests were widely shared, if not universal.

Needless to say, it didn't take long after putting the book down for me to be disabused of that idea. Almost no one around me was interested in spending fifteen minutes a day attaining "cultivation." But this didn't really bother me. I didn't need others to share my interest. After all, one of the great pleasures of reading has always been that it created, long before the advent of Facebook, a virtual community that transcended time and place. What bothered me was my own inability to get past this introduction to the corpus of the Classics.

So the project came to unnerve me as much as it fascinated me. Eventually I found myself turning against Eliot. Old textbooks (and this is how I had come to think of the Harvard Classics: as an enormous old textbook) are strange documents. Because they aspire by their nature to preserve received knowledge for future generations, they often show us a culture at both its most conservative and its most hopeful. As they age, their arguments call out for revision. It becomes tempting to dismiss or even to mock them. This temptation is especially strong in an era like ours, suspicious equally of the future and of the past. While I never reached quite this level of skepticism, I felt a creeping ambivalence toward the Shelf over the course of many summers at that house.

I didn't doubt Eliot's sincerity, exactly. If anything, he seemed too sincere. He was earnest and hopeful in ways that I had learned to distrust, just as I had learned to distrust the sanguine theologians with whom Eliot shared my grandmother's shelves. It all seemed to me—as the past sometimes can't help but seem to us—rather naive. I suspected that the intellectually ambitious families for whom Eliot chose these books—husbands and wives coming home from long days at work to sit down with Emerson or Goethe—had never really existed. This was easier than believing that they had once existed but now were gone—or that perhaps they still did exist, but that I wasn't among them.

★ ★ ★

A few months before that New Year's eve, my aunt Mimi—the second of my grandmother's three daughters—went into the hospital for surgery. She'd had a persistent sore on her foot that had recently been diagnosed as a melanoma, and it was being removed. My mother and my aunt Jaime stayed with her most days while she was there. The office where I worked wasn't far from the hospital, and I walked over to visit them each day during lunch. On one of these days, I brought up the Shelf and my idea about reading through it.

"Mother used to say that she was educated by the Harvard Classics," my own mother said then of my grandmother. "She never got past the eighth grade."

This news startled me. I'd mentioned my interest in these books to my mother before, and it hadn't seemed to move her much one way or another. Perhaps it was the presence of her two older sisters that led her to reveal this connection now. Whatever it was, the three of them were soon reminiscing about their mother while I listened, delighted by the idea that all this time my own family had actually been part of Eliot's audience.

For many years before that day, I had held in my mind two contrasting pictures of my mother's mother, Mary Ryan. One was formed from memories of the brief time that our lives overlapped. I remember a more or less typical grandmother, kind and generous. I remember a woman of devout faith who was also charmingly vain. She lied comically about her age, telling us that she was thirty-nine when she was into her seventies. I remember the long black hair that she wore in a tight bun—hair that I never knew she colored until I went to visit her in the hospital where she lay dying and found it inexplicably gray. More than anything else, what I remember of this version of my grandmother is that one day she was gone, when I'd had no idea that such an absence was possible. It was my first encounter with death, and it found me at an awkward age, when such a thing was just barely comprehensible.

The other long-held image of my grandmother, far more vivid because I remain surrounded by it even now, is of a beautiful woman walking down a runway in Paris with an *haute couture* dress wrapped tightly around her impossibly small waist. In the 1940s and 1950s, my grandmother was a model for Christian Dior. Later in life, she avoided appearing in photographs, as if to ensure the survival of this earlier image.

And so it is: to this day the homes of my mother and my aunt are filled with dozens of pictures of this glamorous figure but almost none of the old woman who abruptly disappeared from my life. When I try to conjure my grandmother now, it is the earlier image that comes reliably to mind, and I suppose this is how she would have wanted it.

But as I listened to that conversation in the hospital, a third image emerged, one that I have since come to feel much closer to. Before her second career as a postwar model or her third as a suburban matriarch, Mary Ryan—then Mary Zielenbach—had been a teenager working in the costume jewelry department at Woolworth's in Elizabeth, New Jersey. At eighteen, she took work in New York's garment district. Through her older sister, she met my grandfather, a former Catholic seminarian who had forgone the priesthood. Through him, she became involved in the bohemian world of Depression-era Greenwich Village.

When they married, my grandparents moved into an apartment on West Twelfth Street. As best I can reconstruct, it was about then that she bought Dr. Eliot's Five-Foot Shelf, perhaps

just around the corner from her apartment on the legendary Booksellers' Row south of Union Square. One way or another, she came to have a set, and she began reading from it. Perhaps she was driven by a desire to fit into the new intellectual world in which she now lived, or perhaps she just read for herself. After a few years, they moved uptown, to the apartment in Morningside Heights where my aunts Jaime and Mimi spent their childhoods. They became friends with intellectual figures from the neighborhood. (There is an old story, an odd piece of family lore, about Lionel and Diana Trilling's son's spitting into my aunt's baby carriage.)

Eventually, my grandfather became sick with tuberculosis and spent time in and out of a sanitarium. In 1947, quite out of financial necessity, my grandmother wound up in the office of Christian Dior. By the time my mother was born, my grandmother had been working as a Dior "mannequin" for several years. Growing up, I often heard stories about an outfit that Dior had designed for the infant Nancy.

Not long after my mother's birth, my grandparents moved the family to a working-class town on Long Island. By this time Jaime was in college and Mimi was in junior high. My grandmother continued to model well into her forties, but the heady days in Manhattan were over. The world in which my mother spent most of her childhood was far removed from the world of New York intellectuals into which she had been born. Still I was shocked at how little I had known of this enviable time in my grandmother's life.

A few days after our conversation at the hospital, I gave my mother a list of the titles in the Harvard Classics. She was herself surprised at how many of these books had remained touchstones for my grandmother throughout her life. She had talked to my mother often of religious writings like Augustine's *Confessions*, *The Imitation of Christ*, and *Pilgrim's Progress*, and also of the fables and tales of Aesop and Grimm. Benjamin Franklin had been a much referenced figure, and my grandmother had told her daughters stories of his life culled from his *Autobiography*.

Speaking with my mother, it struck me how many of the other books on my grandmother's shelves—much of the theology, but also the novels, both "serious" and "light"—might have been arrived at through these early encounters with the Classics. I realized that a woman I had never thought of as especially literary had likely gained from these books a greater grasp on the history of literary culture than her grandson now had.

In one of his few concessions to the potential difficulties of the Classics, Eliot acknowledges in the introduction that "portions" of some volumes make hard reading, mostly because "the sentiments and opinions these authors express are frequently not acceptable to present-day readers." But he concludes that, "It is . . . precisely this encounter with the mental states of other generations which enlarges the outlook and sympathy of the cultivated man."

After hearing these stories about my grandmother, I felt I had been offered the opportunity for a brief encounter with the mental state of a young woman with little formal education but with a sense of "intellectual ambition." My skepticism, my strange resentment toward the Five-Foot Shelf, evaporated. I'd always seen in these books a set of dusty abstractions—enrichment, refinement, cultivation. I saw in them now a meaningful connection to a past I had hardly known existed.

Perhaps I would have come to the point either way, but after that conversation I recommitted myself to the Five-Foot Shelf. It seemed to me that I could spare more than Eliot's suggested fifteen minutes a day of "careful and persistent" reading. In so doing, I might make my way through in rather less than the prescribed several years. Reading roughly a volume a week would allow me to conquer the entire set in a single year. That's what I decided to do.

So I came, at midnight on New Year's eve, to be sitting by myself, reading the first words of the Harvard Classics, on my way to reading the whole five feet.

THE HARVARD CLASSICS

VERI
TAS

SOCRATES

January, or "I Made a Little Book"

Volume I: Franklin; Woolman; Penn
Volume II: Plato; Epictetus; Marcus Aurelius
Volume III: Bacon; Milton; Thomas Browne
Volume IV: *Complete Poems,* Milton

Dear Son—So begins Benjamin Franklin's *Autobiography* (1788), and with it the Harvard Classics. On that New Year's night, the words seemed to confirm my idea of the Classics as a communication from earlier generations, and I was excited to be finally receiving this communication. Several times over the months since I'd come up with my plan to read the Shelf, I'd considered getting an early start. I would walk to the place where the volumes waited in my parents' library and run my fingers along their spines, wondering what secrets they held for me. The fifty-one volumes took up three shelves, each close to two feet wide—the whole thing a bit more than the advertised five feet, I guessed. Reading a volume of four or five hundred pages a week didn't seem like much of a task, but when these books were taken together the expanse was overwhelming.

Now there was nothing to keep me from them. I was ready to read.

But first, I thought I might fix myself a drink—after all, it was New Year's eve. I walked from the library to the kitchen, thinking idly about the contents of this first volume. After Franklin's *Autobiography,* the volume is rounded out by William Penn's *Fruits of Solitude* and the journals of a Quaker named John Woolman. To be honest, I'd questioned the way the Shelf started ever since

I first considered reading it. What was it about these relatively marginal works that earned such a prominent place for them? Why did Eliot start here?

As it happens, I wasn't the first to ask these questions.

Eliot announced his retirement from Harvard in October 1908, to take effect the following May, on the fortieth anniversary of his election to the presidency. A few months after this announcement, two men—William Patten and Norman Hapgood— approached him about editing what became the Classics.

Patten had started in the advertising department at P. F. Collier & Son, where he was the assistant to Condé Nast. He was later moved to the book department, which produced mostly cheap anthologies to be used as inducements for subscribers to *Collier's Weekly*, the muckraking magazine that was the company's major business. (A few years earlier, the magazine had published Upton Sinclair's initial investigations into Chicago's meatpacking industry.) When Patten had the idea of a series of great books that could be offered for subscription, Eliot's name came to mind. Patten proposed his idea to the editor of *Collier's Weekly*, Hapgood, who was an acquaintance of Eliot's. Hapgood assured Patten that there was "not a chance in the world" Eliot would agree to this sort of commercial undertaking. But after Patten produced an old article from *Scribner's Magazine*, in which Eliot had mentioned his long-standing theory about a five-foot shelf that might provide a liberal education, Hapgood agreed to introduce Patten to Eliot. Somewhat to the surprise of both men, Eliot signed on, with the one condition that he be allowed an assistant. For that role, he chose William Neilson, a literature professor at

Harvard who would later become the president of Smith College. Work on the Shelf began almost immediately.

A few weeks into this work, Eliot remarked in a speech given to a high school in Atlanta that he planned to dedicate the early days of his retirement to compiling his Five-Foot Shelf. The news quickly spread that America's most famous educator intended to provide an outline by which any man or woman could attain the best education. It's difficult now to imagine the excitement this announcement generated. Editorials appeared in newspapers around the country. While they waited for Eliot's list to materialize, many of these newspapers invited the presidents of their own local colleges to offer candidates for inclusion. There was a great deal of debate about whether a true education could be had without formal instruction, especially in Latin and Greek.

Initially, Eliot gave no suggestion that his list was part of a business venture, and a number of other publishers—Houghton Mifflin and Funk and Wagnall's among them—approached him with offers to publish his Shelf. Once Collier's involvement became clear, there was suspicion about the project, especially among Harvard alumni, some of whom argued that their university's name—and by extension, its reputation—was being used for personal gain. (In today's age of rampant college licensing, the real surprise is how little compensation Eliot and the university received for their imprimatur: Eliot was given a $2,500 honorarium, which was renewed in later years; Neilson, who did the bulk of the work, was paid $50 a week; the university allowed its name and seal to be used for free.)

In May 1909, well before the selection of the Classics was finished, Collier's salesmen began soliciting subscriptions, using a tentative, incomplete list of titles. This list soon made its way into the press, where it was roundly ridiculed. "Eliot Names

Books for 5-Foot Library," read a headline in the *New York Times* over the subhead, "Shakespeare Is Not in It." On the basis of the odd selection of titles, some newspapers reported that Eliot had been duped into a scheme to unload Collier's underselling backlist. In response to this report and to letters from a number of alumni, Eliot wrote an open letter in the July 7 issue of *Collier's Weekly*.

"The incomplete and inaccurate list which appeared in the newspapers a few weeks ago was issued without my knowledge," he wrote, "and gives an erroneous impression of [the] project." He acknowledged Collier's commercial motives, but he emphasized that his own interest in the project was educational—an assertion that Collier's payment scheme tends to confirm. Eliot also assured readers that he had complete autonomy in choosing the titles for Shelf.

As it happens, this last part wasn't entirely true. The company believed readers would be unlikely to buy a set that included several titles that they already owned—hence the initial exclusion of the Bible and the works of Shakespeare, the two books that any literate household in those days was likeliest to own. This principle also meant excluding nineteenth-century novelists like Dickens and Thackeray, whose works were already offered by Collier. (In the wake of the controversy surrounding the partial list, Eliot would win out on the Bible and Shakespeare, but not on the novels; Dickens and Thackeray would later be included in the Harvard Classics Fiction Shelf, a second set compiled after the great success of the initial Shelf.)

Moreover, the choices that received the most ridicule in the press—Woolman and Penn—had been made before Eliot's involvement in the project even began. Patten put this first vol-

ume together himself as part of his initial proposal to Eliot, who
let the inclusion stand.

I knew very little of this on the night I began reading. Nor did I
know that the volumes had been compiled in more or less ran-
dom order. Like the newspaper columnists of 100 years ago, I
assumed that Eliot had chosen these works to initiate the set for
some good reason. I continued to puzzle over the question after
I sat down with my drink, mostly because it was something to
do besides reading the work that sat open in front of me.

"Dear Son."

The words stopped me as soon as I began. Here in my hands
was a thick old book with an unbroken spine and four hundred
pages. And there on the shelf were fifty more such books. It
didn't seem possible that a year from now the contents of all
those volumes would have passed, however fleetingly, through
my mind. But this wasn't the only problem. The truth is that
as I looked at all those books my whole plan, so fresh just a
moment before, seemed suddenly very silly to me. Perhaps I
wouldn't have felt this way if the Classics had started with
Plato, or Homer, or Shakespeare. But the arbitrary beginning
reminded me of the arbitrary nature of the project. Or better
to say, both projects—Eliot's effort to compile this set and my
effort to read it. What did I hope to achieve with a yearlong
act of literary peak-bagging? Why was I sitting by myself, reading a dead man's letter to his son, instead of celebrating the New
Year with my own family?

But these feelings were dispelled after I forced myself to push
on. Franklin's "letter" occupies about seventy pages, during which

he passes along not just his own life story but his family's history dating back more than a hundred years. He writes about his grandfather, father, and uncles, among them an elder Benjamin Franklin, also something of a man of letters, who liked to transcribe church sermons using, as the younger Franklin writes, "a short-hand of his own, which he taught to me, but, never practicing it, I have now forgot."

Long after Franklin abandons the pretext of the letters, his *Autobiography* maintains its casually paternal tone. For long stretches it forgoes narrative entirely, in favor of simple fatherly advice. Here is the Franklin we all know: Poor Richard with his pithy aphorisms. The man had formed a shorthand of his own— for living—and he was eager that it be practiced and not forgotten. He tells us the thirteen virtues necessary for upright living, beginning with temperance ("Eat not to dullness; drink not to elevation") and ending with humility ("Imitate Jesus and Socrates"). He even explains in practical detail how one can gradually acquire these virtues:

> I judg'd it would be well not to distract my attention by attempting the whole at once, but to fix it on one of them at a time; and, when I should be master of that, then to proceed to another, and so on, till I should have gone thro' the thirteen. . . . I made a little book, in which I allotted a page for each of the virtues. I rul'd each page with red ink, so as to have seven columns, one for each day of the week, marking each column with a letter for the day. I cross'd these columns with thirteen red lines, marking the beginning of each line with the first letter of one of the virtues, on which line, and in its proper column, I might mark, by a little black spot, every fault I found upon

Form of the pages.

TEMPERANCE.						
EAT NOT TO DULNESS; DRINK NOT TO ELEVATION.						
	S.	M.	T.	W.	T.	F.	S.
T.							
S.	*	*		*		*	
O.	**	*	*		*	*	*
R.			*			*	
F.		*			*		
I.			*				
S.							
J.							
M.							
C.							
T.							
C.							
H.							

examination to have been committed respecting that virtue upon that day.

Franklin filled his "little book" with schedules for each day ahead of him and with quotations from Cicero and the Bible. "Tho' I never arrived at the perfection I had been so ambitious of obtaining," he allows, "yet I was, by the endeavor, a better and a happier man than I otherwise should have been." When I read these words in the first hours of the New Year, I imagined making such a book for myself. In it I would schedule out my reading for the months ahead. I'd write down quotations from the Classics that pertained to the perfection I was ambitious of obtaining. (First I would have to figure out what perfection that was.) I'd mark my progress, in reading and living both. Needless to say, I did none of these things. Still, I had recovered, for the time being, from my sinking suspicion that this project wasn't really worthwhile. Franklin's method felt inspirational.

But it didn't feel *literary*. In my years as an undergraduate English major and a graduate student in writing, I'd been taught that good literature wasn't didactic—at least not in such an obvious way. Literature might teach us about life, but it didn't set down rules for daily living in the manner of a self-help book. Yet the first work in the Harvard Classics does just that. This strain is more insistent in some places than in others, more elegant here and less so there, but always present in Franklin's work. If he didn't have something to teach, one senses, he wouldn't have bothered writing at all.

I had thought that "real" literature cared only what kind of reader you were, not what kind of person. But Franklin clearly wanted his readers to think about their life and how it might be better. Of course, the New Year is just the time for such thoughts. But I had already made my resolution—these books were my resolution. Now I was little more than two hours into the year—down the hall I heard my parents returning from their party—and I had the insistent feeling that reading wasn't going to be enough, that what I did after closing the book would matter more.

It had been an unusually warm winter up to that point, but in January the weather turned cold. I was still working part time at the job I was in the process of leaving, and each day in those first weeks of the year I woke up, packed my book into my shoulder bag, and walked in the cold to my office, where I spent the morning doing my work and feeling vaguely out of place. A few of my coworkers who knew I was leaving invited me to good-bye lunches. I accepted each invitation gratefully, but when one o'clock came around I usually made some excuse to put off the lunch to the following week.

Instead I would walk to a restaurant down the block to eat alone and read. After only a few days, the once forbidding red volumes had become amiable companions. The pages were so old and brittle that pieces of them broke off into my lap as I read. I would order a glass of wine, just one, because it helped me to put away the morning's work—the meeting that hadn't gone well; the proposal my boss wasn't happy with—and slip into the world of my reading. At the end of my lunch hour, I'd ask for the check and find that I had been charged for not one but two or three glasses of wine, because as it turned out that's how many I'd had. Then I would stand up and brush the little crumb-like bits of yellowed paper off myself.

As I walked back to work, I found Benjamin Franklin walking along beside me.

"Eat not to dullness," Frankin told me. "Drink not to elevation."

"Shut up, Ben," I answered.

Sometimes it wasn't Ben Franklin but John Woolman or William Penn who tagged along to remind me that I had responsibilities incompatible with drinking three glasses of wine at lunch. By then I had continued along to Woolman's *Journals* (1774) and Penn's *Fruits of Solitude* (1693), works that made me feel even more acutely the difference between literature as I'd known it and what I was reading now.

In writing his introduction to this volume, William Neilson called Woolman "one of America's uncanonised saints." He was a Pennsylvania Quaker, Franklin's contemporary, and a staunch abolitionist in a time when slavery was still prevalent in the northeast and unquestioned by men like Franklin. There's good reason to esteem Woolman as a man, but little to recommend him as a writer. His journals are always admirable and almost always unreadable. They're valuable, I suppose, as historical documents or as the record of an upright life, but not as literature. They have all the didactic fervor of Franklin's *Autobiography* with none of the charm.

The preacherly tendency of the first two works reaches a kind of culmination with the last book of the first volume, William Penn's *Fruits of Solitude*. The book has no narrative whatsoever; it's a collection of maxims for healthy and moral living. A few of them are memorable: "Enquire often, but Judge rarely, and thou wilt not often be mistaken." But after an hour of reading, I would mark my place only to find that twenty pages had passed and I'd absorbed almost nothing at all.

After reading Woolman and Penn, whose status as "Classics" seemed questionable at best, I was relieved to move on to the second volume, which begins with Plato's *Apology, Crito,* and *Phaedo* (c. 375 BCE). Together, these three dialogues make up a kind of passion of Socrates. The *Apology* portrays his trial and sentencing for corrupting Athenian youth. In *Crito*, a young follower attempts to convince Socrates to escape from his cell into exile, which prospect Socrates examines with rational disinterest before abandoning. Last, *Phaedo* recounts Socrates' final moments with his followers before he stoically accepts the hemlock that will kill him. I'd read a good deal of Plato in college, including all three of these works, and I thought I knew what to expect from them. Certainly I had no doubt of their literary merit.

Of course, the dialogues were written—like Franklin's *Autobiography*—to instruct, but this was a different kind of instruction. In one class in college, a reading of *Phaedo* had led to a consideration of Plato's theory of forms. In another, we'd read *Crito* and discussed different notions of justice. These were the sorts of things one expected to learn from such books. And it's true enough that Socrates considers, over the span of these works, justice, metaphysics, and a host of abstractions. But as I read them now, the dialogues seemed quite obviously, at heart, to be concerned with the same question that concerned Franklin and Woolman and Penn: How are we supposed to live?

"A man who is good for anything ought not to calculate the chance of living or dying," Socrates tells the men who stand in judgment of him. "He ought only to consider whether in doing anything he is doing right or wrong—acting the part of a good man or of a bad."

Some days I didn't read at all during my lunch hour but went instead to visit my aunt Mimi, who was recovering from surgery in her apartment, not far from where I worked. I'd stop at a deli down the block and pick up a salad or some soup, and I'd sit beside her bed for half an hour or so. If anything remotely amusing had happened that morning at work, I'd tell her about it. Then she'd tell me about the visitors she'd had since the last time I'd come. Eventually we'd fall silent in the face of all the things we couldn't talk about. Inevitably she'd ask, "How is your reading going?"

"It's going well," I'd say. Or, if I felt like being honest, "I'm not sure."

"You're going to be very smart when this is all over."

"Oh, I know," I'd joke. "I'll be completely insufferable."

This was a common response when people heard about the project I was undertaking. First they would ask how many books were in the Harvard Classics and then, after I'd told them, they would say something about how much I was going to learn, how much I would "know" when the year was over. So I was struck, when I read Plato's dialogues, by the extent to which Socrates insists that his understanding of his own ignorance is the greatest understanding that he has. "I know," he says in the *Apology*, "that I have no wisdom, small or great." As for teaching others, he wants less to teach them new things than to undermine their previously held beliefs.

In the last hours of his life, Socrates discusses the immortality of the soul with his students. They are confident in their own thoughts on the matter, but through his usual combination of sharp questioning and studied irony, Socrates shakes their certainty. "First principles," he tells his students, "even if they appear certain, should be carefully considered; and when they are satisfactorily ascertained, then, with a sort of hesitating confidence in human reason, you may, I think, follow the course of the argument; and if this is clear, there will be no need for any further inquiry."

All the knowledge I might gain from reading these books, Socrates seemed to be telling me, would be worth little beside the knowledge of how little I still knew. Perhaps, I thought, this was what Franklin had had in mind when he urged himself, under the heading of "humility," to imitate Socrates.

In the classroom, we might have evaluated Socrates' self-proclaimed ignorance as a theory of epistemology. But we would never have asked whether it represented a stance worth emulating. Of course, I'd known before I started the Shelf that it contained a different kind of education from the one I'd been given in school. This difference was part of the point. But I hadn't thought much about the nature of the difference. Of what exactly would it consist?

The world that Charles Eliot occupied for most of his life had ideas about education and culture very different from those we hold today. Before New York and then Los Angeles had their turns in the role, nineteenth-century Boston was America's cultural capital, and Harvard was its statehouse. Throughout most of Eliot's years in public life, the country's most prominent cultural critic was his first cousin, Charles Eliot Norton, who had graduated from Harvard University and was a professor there. The country's most famous philosopher was William James, also a professor at Harvard. And its literary forebears, the titans of the previous generation, were Longfellow, who had taught at Harvard and continued to live and write in Cambridge after his retirement from teaching; and Emerson, who had graduated from Harvard and made many of his most famous speeches there.

These were the pillars of what the Spanish-American philosopher George Santayana came to call, somewhat derisively, the "genteel tradition." This tradition understood education and culture as means of personal moral development. It also understood the role of the intellectual elite—the clerisy—as elevating the masses, exposing them to what the British critic

Matthew Arnold called "the best that has been thought and said." Culture upheld the standards and traditions of society at the same time that it helped the individual become a better version of himself.

Charles Eliot was not a scholar of the caliber of Norton or James. He started his career as an instructor of math and chemistry at Harvard, but he was eventually passed over for a professorship. Instead, he was a great educator and popularizer of the ideas of others. And the commercial success of the Harvard Classics suggests that a large part of the American working class believed in this idea of culture and wanted some of it for themselves.

At the time of Eliot's retirement from Harvard, the "genteel tradition" still held sway in this country. But within a few years, after the carnage of World War I, the tradition had largely collapsed. The culture of Modernism, until then confined to a few countries in Europe, exploded on the American scene. The role of the arts was no longer to buttress tradition but to subvert it, to produce a radical break with the past, as the times seemed to demand. Culture began to separate itself into the "high" and the "low." "High" culture was not disseminated from the top down but made by elites for elites. Eliot and other popularizers, who sought to make the best of the cultural tradition more widely accessible, would be derided as "middlebrow."

By the time I started studying literature, this modernist sensibility was itself long outdated. The barrier between high and low culture that erected itself in the last decade of Eliot's life had more or less collapsed. The result was not a return to the genteel, but a broad democratization—what many of Eliot's peers would have called vulgarization. The days when

culture was dispensed by the clerisy to the people for the purpose of internal growth are long gone, and they are unlikely
ever to return.

*First principles, even if they appear certain, should be carefully con-
sidered.* I decided that week to forget, if only for the time being,
what I thought I knew about what literature was, what it was
supposed to look like, and what it was supposed to do. Once I
made this decision, I saw those first volumes, beginning with
Franklin and the defiantly unliterary Woolman, as a kind of
corrective. The earliest parts of the Harvard Classics were trying to turn me into the person I needed to be in order to read
whatever came next. Around the time that I came to this conclusion, I also arrived at the *Meditations* (c. 180 CE) of Marcus
Aurelius, where I read these words:

> Remember how long thou hast been putting off these things,
> and how often thou hast received an opportunity from the
> gods, and yet dost not use it. Thou must now at last perceive
> of what universe thou art a part, and of what administrator
> of the universe thy existence is an efflux, and that a limit of
> time is fixed for thee, which if thou dost not use for clearing
> away the clouds from thy mind, it will go and thou wilt go,
> and it will never return.

As a literary artist, Marcus Aurelius is a substantial improvement on Franklin or Penn. He is even an improvement, I think,
on Plato. But the deepening of beauty in his writing in no way
conceals a slackening of the moral imperative. That a limit of
time is fixed for thee seems to be the overwhelming message of

all his writing. It will go and thou wilt go. But somehow in his hands there is a lightness to this mordant message. He is accepting of the fact in a large-hearted way.

> Lucilla saw Verus die, and then Lucilla died. Secunda saw Maximus die, and then Secundus died. Epitynchanus saw Diotimus die, and then Epitynchanus died. Antoninus saw Faustina die, and then Antoninus died. Such is everything.

Toward the end of the month, Mimi went back into the hospital—her surgery to remove the tumors from her foot had not been completely successful—and so I gave up reading during my lunch hour. Instead, I spent that hour each day in her hospital room. Usually my mother and my aunt Jaime were there, along with one or both of Mimi's sons. There was a single chair in the room and we could usually find a second somewhere down the hall. But that left one or two of us to sit on the floor or scoot Mimi over to share a piece of her bed. We are a family that likes to laugh, even into the void, and that's mostly what we did when we were all together in that room.

In order to keep up, I read a little later than usual at night. I passed on to Francis Bacon, Milton, and Thomas Browne. There was a great deal in all these writers that confused me. But then I read a passage from Browne's *Religio Medici* (1643) that would stay with me throughout the year, even though I never fully understood it.

"Thus is Man that great and true Amphibium," Browne wrote, "whose nature is disposed to live, not onely like other creatures in divers elements, but in divided and distinguished worlds: for though there be but one to sense, there are two to reason, the one visible, the other invisible."

This is how I was already beginning to feel, as though I were living in "distinguished worlds." There was the everyday world around me, and then there was the world of these books. Bacon, Milton, and Browne all seemed to have absorbed the same works that I had read a week earlier. Bacon even makes reference, in his essay *On Friendship* (1601), to Aurelius as an example of "an abundant goodness of nature." This fact added to my sense of a separate world I shared with them, a world where I had a part in an ongoing conversation. And I wanted to be worthy of that world, wanted to bring my very best self to this conversation.

The initial didactic strain of the Classics was already fading, but it had done its work on me. It's difficult to say exactly what had changed. I was still reading to some degree to acquire knowledge, and I was certainly still reading for pleasure. But I was also reading to be a part in a great chain of readers: Aurelius read Plato, then Aurelius died. Milton read Aurelius, then Milton died. And here I sat up in bed reading Milton, fighting off the time when sleep would overtake me. Such is everything.

THE HARVARD CLASSICS

ÆSCHYLUS

February, or "Take Up and Read"

In the Catholic Church in which I was raised, the term "relics of the first degree" refers to actual pieces of a saint: bones or teeth, a strand of hair or a piece of skin preserved over time. Relics of the second degree are objects touched by a saint while he or she lived: tools or clothes or a bishop's mitre. Relics of the third degree are objects that have touched first- or second-degree relics or have simply been blessed in the saint's name. Since the time of the Counter-Reformation, canon law has forbidden the sale of first- and second-degree relics, but third-degree relics, which can be made more or less at will, are available in many churches and religious gift shops. It was such a relic, purchased at the Basilica of Saint Anthony of Padua, that my grandmother—not Mary Ryan but my father's mother, Sanny Beha—gave to me when I got sick.

It's a small, circular thing, a quarter of an inch in diameter, fixed to a piece of paper enclosed in a metal case with a glass front about the size of a nickel. To keep the glass from getting scratched, it's kept in a small felt pouch with a drawstring at the top. My grandmother didn't know, when she gave it to me, that I had already left the Church.

In my early days at college, I'd questioned my faith in a way that many people who are raised in religious households probably do at that age. At times I felt a surprising anger toward the Catholic Church, as if it were all a great lie that had been perpetrated specifically with me in mind. At other times I found it poignantly misguided. But mostly it just left me cold. I went to see a priest who told me that these emotions were quite typical—he'd had them himself—but that I should keep myself open to God's call. I told him I would try to do so.

We were out on Long Island for the summer the first time I stepped back into our pew rather than walking up to the front of the church for Communion. I hadn't said anything to my family about the decision beforehand, and after Mass my parents made their disapproval clear. My mother suspected that I had committed some mortal sin that prevented me from taking the sacrament. She seemed almost relieved when I explained on the drive home that I had simply decided not to do it.

That afternoon I spoke at some length with both of my parents. They realized that I had given much thought to the decision but, like the priest to whom I'd spoken, they wanted me to remain receptive. They worried that cutting myself off from the Eucharist was the wrong way to respond to my doubts. They suggested that skepticism was a game I, as a young man with little responsibility, had the luxury of playing. Many of their own peers, they said, had left the church at about my age, but most had returned eventually, usually at the time when their children were born. If I didn't eventually do the same, it seemed to me, then my parents would consider themselves to have failed in an important way in their lifework, no matter how much else I achieved. As far as I was concerned, these two people had been as near to perfect as possible in raising me, and if I felt any pull back toward religion, it came not from the Church but from a desire to make them happy.

When I went back to college for my junior year, I stopped going to Mass entirely. Around that time, I also started to lose weight—a puzzling but welcome development. Like most of the men in my family, I tend toward bulk, and I had put on some thirty pounds of beer and burgers in my first two years at school. It took a few months of this unexplained slimming before I was down to what I had weighed when I graduated from high school, when I still played competitive sports and didn't drink four nights a week. This should be enough, I thought upon returning to that size, as if I'd been making some effort to shed pounds and could now return to whatever I'd been doing before.

But it wasn't enough: my weight kept dropping. Friends who had complimented me a month earlier now expressed concern. I forced myself to eat more at each meal than the one or two bites it took to fill me up, but this only made me sick afterward. Rumors began to circulate that I had developed an eating disorder. As it happens, this isn't an ailment for which a college-age male will receive much sympathy from other college-age males. Early in my senior year, in a comment book at my eating club, someone wrote the words "Feed Me!" and signed it with my name.

At the same time, I seemed also to be suffering from a persistent case of swollen glands, which made swallowing more difficult and the daily bouts of vomiting even more unpleasant. I was always cold, no matter how many layers of clothing I wore—that is, except at night, when feverish sweats yellowed my sheets. I wasn't sleeping much, but fatigue kept me in bed for much of the day. When I did have the energy to leave my room, I was still reluctant to go out, because I struggled to control my bowels. I threw out four or five pairs of shit-stained boxer shorts a week to avoid the embarrassment of taking them down to the public laundry room. My skin was so dry that it blistered in some places while in others it was moist to the point of fetidness. Each morning I woke with my nose clogged with blood and mucus so thick it could be removed only by hand. And I had a lump the size of a golf ball in my armpit, which made it uncomfortable just to rest my arm at my side.

Taken together, these symptoms so obviously suggest a serious illness that it's difficult now to explain my complacency. But they didn't arrive all at once. They came one at a time, and one at a time I assimilated them into my life. And then the symptoms combined to create an overwhelming malaise that in turn kept me from thinking too deeply into what my problem might be. Now and then I'd go see a doctor in New York, who took cultures from my nose or felt my swollen neck, then prescribed some antibiotics and sent me on my way.

Over the winter break, I went skiing with my family, as I had done all my life. After a day on the slopes my ankles swelled until I could no longer get into my boots. When I returned to school I made an appointment at the infirmary to have them examined. I told the orthopedist about my other symptoms, and he sent me for the X-ray that revealed the tumors in my chest. Only a year before I'd weighed 240 pounds, but at the hospital later that day the scale in the oncologist's office read 163.

In the weeks and months that followed, the news was mostly good. Although the cancer had spread through much of my upper body—I was at stage 3—a bone scan showed no traces in my marrow. A biopsy revealed it to be Hodgkin's lymphoma, which responds better to treatment than the non-Hodgkin's varieties. The doctors felt confident that the chemotherapy would be effective, and they were right. The treatment made me nauseated and tired, but I had already been nauseated and tired for more

than a year, so there was little to complain of. As the cancer re-
treated, most of the symptoms did, too. Within a year I was in
remission.

But in those first days of my diagnosis I knew none of this. I only
knew that I was going to die. I don't mean that I thought my
death was imminent. I understood from the start that a number of things could break in my favor, and I stubbornly expected
that they would. I mean rather that for the first time in my life
I inhabited, from the inside out, the fact of my own mortality.
It was no longer something to be treated objectively; instead, I
had become *its* object. I belonged to it. I had always belonged
to it. This was something wholly new to me, and for a time it
became the central fact—the only fact—of my life.

I don't want to be overly dramatic about this. Most people
are forced into such realizations eventually, and a great many are
forced into them more violently and at a far younger age than I
was. Many people respond by putting themselves in God's hands.
But after I was diagnosed, I knew I would never return to that
kind of faith. Not that I thought I could do without it. On the
contrary, this was the time in my life when I most could have
used the consolation of belief. Perhaps the fact that I couldn't
muster such belief even then proved that it simply wasn't available to me. At any rate, I was certain that I would not be returning to the Catholic Church.

That was when my grandmother gave me her relic. A certain mindset would think it ironic that she should give me this
religious object as a response to the very event that had defini-
tively separated me from my family's religion. The more interesting irony to me is how much the object came to matter to

me—far more, I think, then it would have mattered if I'd still shared her faith. The relic's ostensible meaning rested entirely in a view of the world I could no longer accept. As a third-degree relic, it didn't even have the arbitrary power that attaches itself to rare things. Yet I kept it with me throughout my treatments and for years afterward.

That February—my second month with the Classics—marked the fifth anniversary of my diagnosis. In many ways the one idea I'd been faced with on that day remained the central fact of my life, and the bracing fatalism of Marcus Aurelius was the best answer I'd heard in those five years to the problem posed to me. But I'm writing about all this now not because of that. Or not only because of that. Rather, I'm writing now because I want to tell you about my aunt Mimi.

Her real name was Mary—after her mother—but nearly everyone called her Mimi. She was the younger of my mother's two older sisters, as well as my mother's best friend. She was also my godmother and my confirmation sponsor. She was a physically beautiful woman—like my grandmother, she had worked for a time as a model in Paris. Her husband, my Uncle Michael, died while Mimi was pregnant with her second son, and she raised her two boys by herself. My cousins Paul and Mike are a few years older than my brother and I, but we went to school together and the four of us, along with my older sister, were constant companions.

While I knew her, Mimi taught kindergarten at the Convent of the Sacred Heart on Ninety-First Street, just across Madison Avenue from the town house where I grew up. My mother also taught there, before moving to another school a few blocks away. They were often home together when my brother and I got in from school, and we could hear their laughter from the moment we opened the front door.

Mimi was quicker to laugh than anyone else I've ever known. She could be brought to hysterics over stories she'd heard dozens of times. Anything "suggestive" amused her terribly. Once a connection was drawn between an everyday word and something risqué, one needed only to say the word to get her started. It was the euphemism itself that delighted her so, not the implied naughtiness. I'm sure it would have surprised people who knew her only as a Catholic schoolteacher to hear her scream with laughter over the puerile humor of her sons and her nephews and nieces.

Our families spent summers at my grandmother's house and winter weekends in the Catskills together. At the end of every night, Mimi got down on her knees beside her bed to say the rosary before going to sleep.

She'd had the sore on her foot for a few months and been to several doctors about it by the time the melanoma was diagnosed. By then the cancer was in her bloodstream and there was little hope of containing it. She had surgery to have the growths removed from her foot, in the hope of walking on it again. This is how I came to spend my lunch hours at the hospital that February, instead of in a restaurant by myself, and how I came to put my reading off until late at night.

I continued to visit her several times a week after I left my office job. I'd already moved in with my parents from my apartment downtown. I was doing some freelance writing, but I had all the time I needed for my books. I was sitting in my parents' library toward the end of that month, reading Saint Augustine's *Confessions* (397), when the phone rang. I had just reached the point in Book Four when Augustine, then a Manichean, loses his closest friend. "My life was a horror to me," he writes, "because I would not live halved."

> O madness, which knowest not how to love men, like men! O foolish man that I then was, enduring impatiently the lot of man! I fretted then, sighed, wept, was distracted; had neither rest nor counsel. For I bore about a shattered and bleeding soul, impatient of being borne by me, yet where to repose it, I found not.

I left the book open on my lap while I answered the phone. The man at the other end of the line asked to speak with one of my parents. When I told him they weren't home, he gave his name. He was Mimi's doctor. I sensed that he had important news. At any rate, he didn't seem satisfied with just leaving a message.

"I'm Chris," I told him. "We met at the hospital."

"Yes," he acknowledged in a noncommittal tone.

"I'm familiar with Mimi's case," I added.

This seemed to satisfy him.

"We've got the results of Mary's scan," he told me. In all my life, I'd only heard a few people call her Mary. "We've found two lesions on her brain."

"OK," I said.

"We're going to try some radiation and see if they respond at all."

"OK."

"I've already told Mary this myself," he explained. "But I'm not sure how much of it she took in. I wanted to make sure that your family understood the situation."

"Thank you," I said. "I'll be sure to speak with everyone."
The first thing I felt after hanging up was surprise that he had been willing to give me this information over the phone. Of course, this was precisely what I'd meant to encourage when I'd rather awkwardly told him that I was "familiar" with Mimi's "case." I wondered whether he was even allowed to reveal private information about a patient's condition. I have a few friends who are doctors, and I decided I would ask one of them exactly what the standards were in such cases. I marked my page in Augustine's *Confessions* and closed the book. I wondered which of my doctor friends I should ask about this issue of privacy. It felt very important in that moment to find out whether I was permitted to know that the doctors had decided to radiate my Aunt Mimi's brain.

I called my mother on her cell phone. She told me she was in Mimi's hospital room. She'd spoken with the doctor after I'd gotten off the phone with him. I told her I'd be over soon, and I hung up. If I'd spoken with my mother, and she'd spoken with the doctor in front of Mimi, then I was now allowed to have the information the doctor had given me. This relieved me a little, and in that moment I started to understand the meaning of what I had been told. Then I cried for the next five or ten minutes, in a snuffly, sobbing way that I hadn't cried for some time. When I was through, I went to the dresser in my bedroom and took out my relic of Saint Anthony of Padua.

When I got to the hospital, my mother, my aunt Jaime, and my cousin Michael, Mimi's younger son, were all in the room together. Mimi was awake but not sitting up. I went to her, held her hand, and kissed her cheek. I told her that I'd brought her the relic my grandmother had given me when I was sick, and I placed it in its little felt pouch on the tray beside her bed. She pulled me close and whispered in my ear.

"I'm scared," she said to me.

"I know," I said.

I'd spent the first week of February reading Ralph Waldo Emerson, the intellectual godfather of the New England–Victorian genteel tradition that Eliot exemplified. The two men were separated by hardly more than a generation (Emerson graduated from Harvard in the 1820s, Eliot in 1853), and Eliot considered Emerson one of the greatest men in human history. The inclusion of a figure from roughly one's own time and place on such a list of books is itself an Emersonian gesture, for one of Emerson's credos was "The sun shines to-day also."

Like Eliot—like Plato, like Franklin—Emerson was deeply concerned with education. He articulated as eloquently as anyone ever has the belief in education and culture as methods of personal development and moral uplift. The first of Emerson's essays included in the Five-Foot Shelf, "The American Scholar," was originally delivered at Harvard in the 1830s, and it had no precedent in American literature. The very idea that there could be such a species as an American scholar, that he could have traits and tendencies that separated him from the European variety, was wholly new. Still, Emerson appreciated the value of the past, particularly as it is given to us in books. "The theory of books is noble," Emerson wrote. He continued:

The scholar of the first age received into him the world around; brooded thereon; gave it the new arrangement of his own mind, and uttered it again. It came into him life; it went out from him truth. It came to him short-lived actions; it went out from him immortal thoughts. It came to him business; it went from him poetry. It was dead fact; now it is quick thought. It can stand and it can go. It now endures, it now flies, it now inspires. Precisely in proportion to the depth of mind from which it issued, so high does it soar, so long does it sing.

As someone who had given himself over to reading books, I was naturally inspired by this ideal. But Emerson adds a warning. "Each age," he insists, "must write its own books; or rather, each generation for the next succeeding." It's not that older books are no longer valuable, but as they age—as they become "Classics"—we become too respectful of them; we stop seeing them for what they are: "Meek young men grow up in libraries believing it their duty to accept the views which Cicero, which Locke, which Bacon have given, forgetful that Cicero, Locke, and Bacon were only young men in libraries when they wrote these books."

At the time I read these words, it would have been possible for me to spend entire days without moving from that library, doing nothing but reading the books of an older period. And some days I did. But mostly I didn't—not because I didn't enjoy it there, but because reading someone like Emerson is bound to send you back out into the world.

I don't know why this surprised me so much. Throughout my life, I'd experienced the familiar sensation of getting lost in books, but these books wouldn't let me lose myself. For Emerson the first great influence on the scholar, before books, must be the world itself: "Every day, the sun; and, after sunset, Night and her stars. Ever the winds blow; ever the grass grows. Every day, men and women, conversing, beholding and beholden. The scholar is he of all men whom this spectacle most engages."

Now, when I looked up from the page, I saw a world very different from Emerson's. I don't mean simply that I was in a modern city where little grass grew. I don't mean simply that I found in our contemporary culture an abiding emptiness that would have disappointed all of Emerson's hopes for us. And I don't mean simply that I found our political moment at once dangerous and mindless in ways that made me want to stop paying attention to it. All this was true, but I was bothered by something deeper. Here is Emerson's scholar, looking at the world:

These objects are not chaotic, and are not foreign, but have a law which is also a law of the human mind . . . Thus to him, to this school-boy under the bending dome of day, is suggested that he and it proceed from one root; one is leaf and one is flower; relation, sympathy, stirring in every vein. And what is that Root? Is not that the soul of his soul? A thought too bold, a dream too wild. Yet when this spiritual light shall have revealed the law of more earthly natures, when he has learned to worship the soul, and to see that the natural philosophy that now is, is only the first gropings of its gigantic hand, he shall look forward to an ever-expanding knowledge as to a becoming creator.

But this wasn't my experience. That a woman should work all her life to raise two sons, only to become mortally ill just as they were old enough and successful enough to help her in turn; that a woman not only kind but devout should be so mistreated by life—these facts offered no "law of more earthly natures." If the visible world suggested the gropings of a gigantic hand, then the intelligence attached to this hand was clumsy or malicious, or else it simply didn't exist.

Emerson was saying that our understanding of the creator, not the creator itself, was flawed. But this view demanded that one derive from nature the concept of a creator, only then to derive from one's conception of that creator a more perfect idea of nature. I couldn't accept this circular process from such a powerful mind. The world as I experienced it in those months, as I had experienced it throughout those five years, was unordered—or else ordered by malevolent forces. Yet throughout that time, there was the relic. A tiny piece of darkened tin, stuck in a case and sold at a markup. And there I was giving it to her.

I wanted to believe, at the most basic level, that there was order to the world, but I couldn't believe that this order was all good. After reading the *Confessions*, I suspected that a similar dilemma had led Saint Augustine to leave the Catholic Church in which his mother had raised him, and led him to the practice of Manichaeism. The belief that the world represents not the creation of a benevolent and omnipotent God but a battle of imperfectly powerful forces of light and of darkness was widely held during the early Christian era in which Augustine lived. Augustine abandoned that belief eventually, only to move on to a belief in astrology and a series of other heresies. In all that time, he was tugged back toward the Church by the same force—family—that still tugged me toward it, despite everything else I felt.

Augustine's *Confessions* is often described as the world's first autobiography, and it may be that. But it is also the record of a devout woman's disappointment over her son's lack of faith—"My mother, thy faithful one, weeping to Thee for me, more than mothers weep the bodily deaths of their children." Augustine's mother fears dreadfully for his soul. Among other things, she bitterly regrets allowing him to be educated in Latin

and Rhetoric, to read Cicero and other Romans. His learning—
his books—led him astray.

But in the end, Augustine tells us, his books as much as the
love of his mother bring him back. When he reads the Greeks,
especially Plato, he learns about the hidden order of the world,
and this prepares him to read Saint Paul, whose influence will
be definitive. This last step requires a bit of intervention from
the outside world. Augustine is "weeping in the most bitter con-
trition" when he hears a child's voice in the neighboring house,
repeating the phrase, "Take up and read; take up and read." He
returns to Saint Paul.

> I seized, opened, and in silence read that section on which my
> eyes first fell: Not in rioting and drunkenness, not in chamber-
> ing and wantonness, not in strife and envying; but put ye on
> the Lord Jesus Christ, and make not provision from the flesh,
> in concupiscence. No further would I read; nor needed I: for
> instantly at the end of this sentence, by a light as it were of
> serenity infused into my heart, all the darkness of doubt van-
> ished away.

I read these words that night after I got back from the hospital. Part of me envied Augustine the disappearance of his doubt.
But remembering Emerson, I also thought: even Saint Paul was
just a man who wrote those words.

By the end of February, Mimi had been discharged from the
hospital, but she could no longer live on her own. She was
wheelchair-bound. She needed help getting into and out of bed,
and she needed someone to bring her back to the hospital each

day for radiation. Her older son Paul lived downtown and her younger son Mike was in law school. So she moved into my parents' apartment, just as I had done a few weeks before.

At the time that Mimi moved in, I was reading Aeschylus in the volume of Greek drama. The three plays that make up his *Oresteia* (458 BCE)—*Agamemnon, The Libation Bearers,* and *The Furies*—represent the closest surviving thing to one of the dramatic tetralogies that were performed at the Greek festivals (the only missing element is the satyr play that would typically close out the performance). They also express more perfectly than any other intact work the Greeks' peculiar tragic sense.

The first of the plays begins with Agamemnon's triumphant return to his home in Argos from the Trojan War. In order to appease the gods and ensure victory in Troy, Agamemnon had been forced to sacrifice his daughter Iphigenia. Now, he brings to Argos the Trojan prophetess, Cassandra, whom he has been given as a spoil of war. Cassandra sees that he will punished for his daughter's death:

Home cursed of God! Bear witness unto me,
Ye visioned woes within—
The blood-stained hands of them that smite their kin—
The strangling noose, and, spattered o'er
With human blood, the reeking floor!

Sure enough, Agamemnon's wife Clytemnestra slays both him and Cassandra. Although Clytemnestra acts in part to avenge her daughter's sacrifice, her motives are decidedly mixed: she has taken a lover, Aegisthus, in her husband's absence, and Aegisthus wishes to usurp the throne. After killing Agamemnon, the two lovers rule Argos together.

In the second play, *The Libation Bearers*, Agamemnon and Clytemnestra's surviving children, Orestes and Electra, seek to avenge their father's death by killing Clytemnestra. Matricide is a much graver crime than killing one's spouse, as the two children know, because it is a crime against a direct blood relation. But the plotters are urged on by Apollo and by the oracle. Here is the fatalism that is such a central component of Greek tragedy. Just as Agamemnon had no choice but to sacrifice Iphegenia, Orestes knows what he is bringing on himself even as he carries out his plan:

> The slayer of today shall die tomorrow—
> The wage of wrong is woe.
> While Time shall be, while Zeus in heaven is lord,
> His law is fixed and stern;
> On him that wrought shall vengeance be outpoured—
> The tides of doom return.
> The children of the curse abide within
> These halls of high estate—
> And none can wrench from off the home of sin
> The clinging grasp of fate.

In the last play in the trilogy the Furies, pre-Olympian deities responsible for maintaining moral order, hunt down Orestes. He seeks refuge with Apollo, who had led him to his crime. Apollo sends him to Athens, where the Furies track him down. There he is under the protection of Athena, who tries to persuade the Furies to let Orestes live. She brings in a group of Athenian citizens to serve as jurors and hold an impromptu trial, in which Orestes is acquitted. Throughout this scene, the Chorus, representing the older order of gods, repeats these lines:

Woe on you, younger gods! the ancient right
Ye have o'erridden, rent it from my hands.

Taken as a whole, the *Oresteia* can be read as the story of a
shift in the moral order, a change in the conception of justice
on earth that is mirrored by a change in the heavens, where the
Olympian gods wrest control from the Titans. This is the movement toward the particular kind of democratic order for which
the Athenians are famous. The stories of the Trojan War, taken
by the Greek dramatists mostly from Homer, were already hundreds of years old by the time Aeschylus wrote in the fifth century BCE. When Aeschylus wanted to give a picture of Athenian
culture, he located it at this moment, when one order passed
away and another took its place.

Just as Emerson says that each age needs its own books,
Aeschylus seems to say that each age needs its own gods, that
each age makes its own order. But this doesn't mean that the
old books or the old gods no longer matter. On the contrary, it
is a reason to read those books and study those gods, not to discover the order of the world, but precisely because there is no
order except the one we make.

The important point was that other people, long before, had
wrestled with the same problems that troubled me. They had
created solutions for themselves and then set these solutions
down in the hope that they would last. Their answers could not
be my answers, but it mattered that we struggled together, each
in our ways. Thus, my grandmother's gift meant one thing to
her and another to me, but it mattered to both of us, and that
much we shared.

When I told my friends at different times throughout the year
about the reading I was doing, some of them wondered aloud

how much history really has to tell us about technology, terrorism, and everything else that makes our age unprecedented. They seemed to find my project charming but ultimately inexplicable, as if a thousand-year-old book couldn't possibly meet the particular problems of the modern era.

But my problems didn't seem all that particular to the modern era. The people I loved were going to suffer, and so was I. Then they would be gone, and eventually so would I. Reading these words that others had set down while they suffered and before they were gone made things easier for me. *Relics*, my friends might have said. I would have answered: precisely—for they have been touched by the saints.

THE HARVARD CLASSICS

VERITAS

CICERO

March, or "Not By the Knowledge of Words"

I'm sitting in the dark beside my five-year-old nephew Peter, watching galaxies collide. They twirl toward each other gracefully, almost shyly, like would-be lovers in a cartoon or an old musical, and then they kiss ever so lightly and go off in surprising directions, breaking apart as they do. The familiar, soothing voice of Robert Redford explains that we're watching our own galaxy, the Milky Way, and our nearest neighbor, Andromeda. The collision is taking place 3 billion years from now. The sight is so beautiful that it's hard to comprehend the fact that we're watching the destruction of everything we've ever known.

Perhaps Peter understands this meaning better than I do, because he squirms a little in the seat next to me. He asks in a whisper if we can leave. I hold his hand and tell him it will be over in a minute. Above our heads, the show moves on to other celestial bodies crashing into one another.

Afterward, we stand outside with smiles on our faces. Peter's worry has evaporated; the spectacle has won out.

"Pretty cool," I say.

"Yeah," he affirms. "Pretty cool."

"Now let's go look at the dinosaurs."

Peter is the oldest of my sister Alice's children. He's precocious and endlessly curious, and he's very much an outer space guy. He's one of those kids who know, as if born knowing, not only the order of the planets but which ones have moons and rings and how many. Myself, I've always been a little over-whelmed by the cosmos; if I think too long about space I start to squirm, as Peter did inside the planetarium. I've brought him crosstown to the Museum of Natural History to see this light show. But in truth, I'm here for the bones.

The week before our trip, I read Darwin's *On the Origin of Species* (1859). Actually, it may be an overstatement to say that I *read* all of it, but I can say with some confidence that my eyes passed over every word. I'm willing to concede that this state of affairs wasn't entirely Charles Darwin's fault; by the middle of March I was suffering slightly from Classics fatigue. Needless to say, this worried me a bit, since I was still less than a quarter of the way through the Shelf.

My problems had begun at the beginning of the month, with Cicero. Not that I disliked Cicero's writing. Some of it I liked very much. He writes with great charm and intelligence, and he's often quite funny. Here he is in his essay "On Old Age" (65 BCE):

> For my part, I know not only the present generation, but their fathers, also, and their grandfathers. Nor have I any fear of los-ing my memory by reading tombstones, according to the vul-gar superstition. On the contrary, by reading them I renew my memory of those who are dead and gone. Nor, in point of fact, have I ever heard of any old man forgetting where he had hid-den his money. They remember everything that interests them.

But I felt when reading Cicero that I was missing some essential part of what made this writer so important. A note in the editor's introduction explains that Cicero was best known as the "great forensic and political orator of his time." Of the many speeches he made throughout his public life, fifty-eight survive. The introduction reports that these works "bear testimony to the skill, wit, eloquence, and passion which gave [Cicero] his preeminence." But none of them are included here. Eliot and Neilson decided, quite correctly, I'm sure, that they wouldn't mean much to the common reader who made up the Classics' target audience. Each speech is too bound up in the particular moment—whether murder trial or political dispute—that occasioned it. So the works included in the Harvard Classics—his treatises *On Friendship* and *On Old Age*, as well as many of his letters—are not the ones that primarily made Cicero's reputation.

This was only part of my difficulty in appreciating Cicero. I asked my sister Alice, who had majored in Classics in college, about Cicero, and she confirmed that he was the great master of Latin prose. Most of his appeal, she explained, rested in this fact. In her opinion, it wasn't something that could be easily conveyed in translation.

I'd given some thought to the problem of translation before starting my reading of the Five-Foot Shelf. Because my initial interest in the project was so tied to the books themselves—that is, to the books as *objects*—there was never any question of seeking out modern editions. I wasn't going to read the Penguin Classics or the Modern Library Classics; I was going to read the

Harvard Classics. For better or worse, this meant carrying around these red hardcovers, with their fragile spines and brittle pages. At times it meant doing physical damage to objects that I'd made into something of a fetish. And it meant reading the translations that Eliot and Neilson had chosen.

There were weeks when this limitation was especially frustrating—for instance, when I arrived at the Elizabethan translation of Montaigne, I hardly recognized the essayist I'd fallen in love with at college. At other times it seemed fitting—even though I wanted to read Robert Fagles's recent rendering of the *Aeneid,* John Dryden's seventeenth-century version is itself a classic.

The Five-Foot Shelf appeared at a time when most educated people still had some grip on classical languages. When Eliot announced that the Shelf would be entirely in English, several commentators remarked that it must be aimed at an audience without even a few years of formal education. But as Eliot notes in his introduction, publishing all the works in English was central to the project's mission, which was to make the great products of human thought available to any interested American reader. "With such objects in view," Eliot wrote, "it was essential that the whole series should be in the English language; and this limitation to English necessitated the free use of translations, in spite of the fact that it is impossible to reproduce perfectly in a translation the style and flavor of the original." He concludes, "Nevertheless, translations can yield much genuine cultivation to the student who attends to the substance of the author's thought, although he knows all the time that he is missing some of the elegance and beauty of the original form."

Eliot is quite right that translation need not be an insurmountable hurdle. The letters of Pliny the Younger appear in the same volume as these works by Cicero, and I didn't struggle in this way with them. I suspect this is because their value rests more on what Eliot would call their "substance" rather than their "flavor." They give a wonderful sense of life in the early days of the Roman empire, and of the personality of Pliny himself. "You will laugh (and you are quite welcome)," he writes to one of his friends, "when I tell you that your old acquaintance is turned sportsman, and has taken three noble boars."

"What!" you exclaim, "Pliny!"—Even he. However, I indulged at the same time my beloved inactivity; and, whilst I sat at my nets, you would have found me, not with boar spear or javelin, but pencil and tablet, by my side. I mused and wrote, being determined to return, if with all my hands empty, at least with my memorandums full.

But the problem in Cicero's case is far more acute. For hundreds of years, nearly up to the time of the Harvard Classics themselves, formal education in Christian nations revolved around the so-called trivium: Latin, logic, and rhetoric. Disciplines such as arithmetic and music rounded out the curriculum, but the trivium came first. And in this model, Cicero—the master of Latin prose who was also a master of logic and rhetoric—was one of the two or three truly essential writers.

As I read his letters, I was constantly reminded that their greatest virtue—the "elegance and flavor" of the Latin prose—was unavailable to me. By definition, of course, I couldn't know what I was missing. But when I read, for example, the passage where Cicero tells his brother Quintus, "In your Manilian property I came across Diphilus outdoing himself in dilatoriness," I couldn't help wondering if this perfectly serviceable construction, with its able use of alliteration and assonance, wasn't something sublime in the original. But I had no way to tell. To use a metaphor that Cicero, as the man who introduced Greek philosophy to the Romans, might appreciate, I was looking at the shadows of his writing against the wall of the cave; I couldn't see outside to where the thing itself stood.

Perhaps this need not have caused any great crisis. After all, it wasn't the first time I hadn't been moved as much as I might have been by my reading. (Certainly, I enjoyed Cicero's letters better than I had John Woolman's *Journals*.) But there was an important distinction here. It wasn't merely that I didn't fully appreciate Cicero, but that I *couldn't* fully appreciate him, because the Cicero who had earned his place in the Harvard Classics wasn't actually there on the page.

One fundamental premise of the Five-Foot Shelf is that the great monuments of the past—and, by extension, the past itself—are available to us. We don't need experts to make sense of them; we don't need years of training to unlock their secrets. We need only do as Augustine did: take up and read. But as I struggled to appreciate Cicero, I wondered if this was always the case.

I supposed the best solution would have been to learn Latin and read him in the original. I actually had taken a few semesters of the language in college, but I never got anywhere with it. And in any case, I also lacked what the introduction to this volume called "a full knowledge of the history, political and personal, of the time." Even if I learned this history (so my thinking went in these days in early March), there would always be something else to prevent me from a full reckoning with the meaning of the work.

For centuries, learning Cicero had been a rite of passage for schoolboys. But when my sister graduated with her degree in

Classics, there were only four other seniors in her department. Allowing for majors in history, literature, and archaeology who might have known some Latin, there can't have been more than a few dozen students in a class of 1,000 who could have read Cicero with the sort of pleasure he had once provided. There are only a few nonspecialists left to whom this pleasure is available, and there must be fewer in each generation. It seemed to me that if Cicero had survived for twenty centuries mostly because he exemplified the Latin and Rhetoric that were central to a certain method of education, he was unlikely to survive much longer than the method itself. Perhaps by the end of the twenty-first century most educated people won't even have heard of him.

Of course, this isn't a wholly regrettable possibility. The battle to end classical education was hard fought (Charles Eliot was among those who fought it), and the victory has done us great service. Whenever I become nostalgic for the old system, I remind myself that if my culture spent most of its educational resources on Latin, it might never have developed the cancer treatments that saved my life. But there is also a cost—a loss of continuity—and a project like the Harvard Classics can never entirely redress it.

Perhaps this complaint sounds academic, but it didn't feel that way to me. Since Mimi had moved in, I was spending most of the day with her. In the morning, I would wheel her into the library, where she would read magazines while I worked my way through Cicero. When it came time for her radiation treatment, my parents or my aunt Jaime would usually take her. But twice when the others were busy I wheeled her down the big hill that slopes below the Queensborough Bridge to the complex of hospitals along the river.

During these trips I spoke with her about my own radiation treatments, which had gone on only a month but had given me a sunburn that seemed to last half the year. We also talked about my reading and about the book I hoped to write. I told her that I couldn't imagine writing about this year without writing a good deal about her and what she was going through, and I wanted to make sure she felt comfortable with being included.

"Of course," she said. Although I was walking behind her wheelchair, I could picture the smile on her face from the tone in her voice. "You're going to make me famous."

Hearing the pleasure in her voice at this idea was one of my happiest moments. For the few blocks we had left on our route and all the way back up the hill afterward, I allowed myself to think that, no matter what happened to Mimi (and I still had hope that everything would turn out all right), I could save her in some way if I got everything down just right on the page. I knew the idea was fanciful, perhaps even arrogant, but it was too beautiful to give up. Until then, my reading had encouraged the thought.

So you see, I had a real stake in the question that these translations of Cicero had raised. I needed the past to be available to us, to be accessible on the page, even generations later. It discouraged me to see that this wasn't always so.

Mimi's moving in had been proposed as a temporary solution, but the unspoken assumption was that she would stay on after her radiation was finished. This is indeed what happened. In those days she was still mentally active, even though her mobility was limited. In the morning, my mother or my father or I would help her from her bed into her wheelchair, and then wheel her into the library or into my parents' bedroom to watch television. The fact that I had been forced to move back in with my parents, the fact that I spent so much of my time sitting around and reading, had seemed until then like something of an embarrassment. Now it felt like a blessing. My presence allowed my mother to leave the apartment when she needed to run errands. It allowed for an extra pair of hands when something (or someone) needed lifting.

Above all, it allowed me to see much more of Mimi than I would have otherwise. Twice a week when her physical therapist arrived, I would help Mimi into the hallway, which she would make her way up and down in a walker before falling back into her chair in exhaustion. I would be there to encourage her. I would tell her how proud I was of how hard she was working. And she would tell me how it helped to hear that, which I hoped was also true.

In those days I often had to choose between spending the afternoon sitting with her, watching *A Fish Called Wanda* or an old Preston Sturges comedy, or reading another sixty pages of the Classics. This was no choice at all. In the evenings and on weekends my cousins Mike and Paul came to see their mother, usually along with Mike's fiancée Emily, my twin brother Jim, and Jim's fiancée Alyson. Then we would all sit together for hours and enjoy the feeling of common purpose that has always seemed the chief consolation of difficult times. All this meant that in those days I read late at night, after most of the family had left and Mimi had taken her sleeping pills and been helped back to bed.

These late nights of reading coincided with my arrival at the two books—Adam Smith's *Wealth of Nations* (1776) and Darwin's *On the Origin of Species*—that felt most like textbooks, or most like assigned reading. This coincidence made the project begin to feel like cramming for a test of my own devising.

Very early in the year, I had circled these volumes where they appeared beside each other on the list of the Classics. I was apprehensive about these two books, but I was also excited about them. When one thinks of "great books," one generally thinks of the humanities. But Charles Eliot was a chemist and mathematician by training, and he understood the importance of the sciences, though he lived before the great explosion of technology that marked the twentieth century. One thing I liked about the Shelf was that it included these central texts of economics and evolutionary biology.

Many of my friends in college were economics majors, and many of those who weren't still wound up working as bankers, traders, management consultants. I never took a single economics course, and my lack of even a rudimentary understanding of the discipline has always bothered me. So I looked forward to reading *Wealth of Nations*. In this book, Adam Smith first explained the field's basic principles. The volume offered a tangible kind of knowledge. It is difficult to articulate, after reading Aeschylus, precisely what one has "learned." But after reading *Wealth of Nations,* I could tell you any number of things—about labor, capital, trade, pricing, profit, supply, and demand—previously unknown to me.

I had worried that Smith's work would require some background in economics. But the discipline hardly existed before *Wealth of Nations.* The book assumes that the reader knows little or nothing about the study of economics, because little or nothing was known about it before Smith explained it. For this reason, I was perhaps a better reader than some of my friends who knew the field well.

After this experience, I expected much the same of *On the Origin of Species*. It too was the founding text of an entire discipline, a book that I wanted to read (or at least wanted to have read), but one I could hardly imagine picking up without the prompting of this project. It was just the kind of book, in other words, for which I'd begun reading the Shelf in the first place. And it began well enough. The premise, by now universally known, is laid out with admirable clarity in the first pages.

"Until recently," Darwin writes, "the great majority of naturalists believed that species were immutable productions, and had been separately created. This view has been ably maintained by many authors. Some few naturalists, on the other hand, have believed that species undergo modification, and that the existing forms of life are the descendents by true generation of the pre-existing forms." He goes on to provide the strongest case that had yet been made for the latter belief, and to offer his own theory of natural selection as the means by which these "modifications" take place. I have been told by some friends of mine who work in the field that what follows is the most exhilarating work of scientific argument in human history. Unfortunately, long stretches of it might as well have been written in Cicero's Latin.

I suspect that this can't really be helped. On more than one occasion, Darwin shows that he is capable of wonderfully lively and thoughtful prose. "It may metaphorically be said," he writes, "that natural selection is daily and hourly scrutinising, throughout the world, the slightest variations; rejecting those that are bad, preserving and adding up all that are good; silently and insensibly working, whenever and wherever opportunity offers, at the improvement of each organic being in relation to its organic and inorganic conditions of life. We see nothing of these slow changes in progress, until the hand of time has marked the lapse of ages, and then so imperfect is our view into long-past geological ages, that we see only that the forms of life are now different from what they formerly were."

But in the end, he is making an empirical argument, and he is making that argument to the scientific community, which means that the common reader is left behind for large stretches at a time. Thus, passages like the ones quoted above are far less common than passages like this:

Finally, then, I conclude that the greater variability of specific characters, or those which distinguish species from species, than of generic characters, or those which are possessed by all the species; that the frequent extreme variability of any part which is developed in a species in an extraordinary manner in comparison with the same part in its congeners; and the slight degree of variability in a part, however extraordinarily it may be developed, if it be common to a whole group of species; that the great variability of secondary sexual characters, and their great difference in closely allied species; that secondary sexual and ordinary specific differences are generally displayed in the same parts of the organisation,—are all principles closely connected together.

This sentence makes perfect sense. It's not loaded down with scientific jargon. But such sentences aren't exactly well suited to being read late at night after long and emotionally draining days. This is why, by the time I went with my nephew Peter to the Museum of Natural History, I had passed my eyes over every word in *On the Origin of Species*, but I couldn't honestly say that I'd read it.

Before heading in to look at the dinosaur bones, we stopped to watch a short film about the evolution of species. A voice

slightly less familiar than Robert Redford's—it belonged to the
star of a television show—told us that each species, like each individual creature, struggles for survival and must eventually die
out. Then the voice explained what the fossil record can teach
us about life before the evolution of humans, including possible
mass extinctions in which large numbers of species were wiped
out at one go. The voice added that one species had been responsible for more of these extinctions in the past hundred years than
had occurred in thousands of years before.

"Which species is that?" Peter asked me.

"Us," I said.

"Oh."

Watching this movie so soon after the light show, I was
struck by how much we'd been able to learn, through digging
in the ground and looking up into the sky, about what the
world was like before we came to be and what it will be like
after we've ceased to be. That we had, on such a grand scale,
some sense of where we'd come from and where we were
heading was itself a kind of miracle, even if the answer to both
questions was "extinction."

I walked with Peter through the Hall of Fossils. I'm the
youngest child in my family, and there were no babies around
for most of my life, so Peter's arrival represented an important
change for me. He seems to me still a great wonder, and it was
a thrill to see his own sense of wonder at the spectacle of these
giant creatures that lived and then died out long before us. I don't
know how much my reading of Darwin, such as it was, informed
my trip through those halls. I think it would make more sense
to say that my trip to the museum informed my reading. In the
days that followed, I went back over the book, and I was struck
more by the brief moments of eloquent synthesis than by the

long stretches of tedium. (I won't pretend that those stretches were no longer there.)

Before we left the museum, Peter and I went to the gift shop to buy a souvenir for him and a few things to bring to his brother and sisters. Then we took the bus back crosstown to my parents' apartment, where my sister Alice and the rest of her children were visiting with Mimi. Peter burst in, loud with the excitement of his outing, and his siblings responded with equal excitement when they saw the rubber dinosaurs we'd brought for them. But my sister looked stricken.

Because her three younger children were not yet of school age and her husband worked long hours, Alice hadn't been here to see Mimi as often as she wanted, and she was surprised by Mimi's condition. Seeing her for a moment through Alice's eyes, I was surprised myself. She'd lost more weight than I'd realized; her face had grown thinner; and her hair, which had also been thinned by the radiation, had gone gray in the past few weeks.

"She looks like grandma," Alice told me.

In fact, Mimi had always looked like her mother—they had both been models and were both quite beautiful. But Alice meant that this woman in her early sixties looked as Mary Ryan had looked at the end of her life, when she was in her late seventies, dying of cancer.

Though I had been unwilling or unable to express it, the same thought had come to me about a week earlier, on a day when my mother's cousins had come to visit Mimi. One of them had brought a written history of my grandmother's family, the Zielenbachs. The history went back into the 1800s, and included names I'd never seen. As I looked at this sheet, I thought of some of the charts included in Darwin's book, which track the progression of all life over aeons but otherwise look like family trees.

I had the terrible feeling then that Mimi was receding into the past, that one day she would be one of the names on her cousin's sheet, a woman born two hundred years ago.

When Alice brought the idea to me again after my trip to see the fossils, I thought: we are all retreating. I expected the idea to scare me, but it comforted me instead. We would continue our retreat until we were no longer even names, but mere letters on some future scientist's charts. Or we would go toward the vanishing point, until we reached the very origin, and all of life would stretch out ahead of us, and none of it would be ours.

Somehow that day shook me out of the fatigue I had felt with regard to my reading. I returned to Darwin with renewed interest for a few days before moving on to Plutarch's *Lives* (c. 100 CE). Plutarch was a Greek who lived during the early days of the Roman empire. His great work, *Parallel Lives of the Noble Greeks and Romans*, contains pairings of Greeks and Romans whose stories seem to inform each other. In many cases, they are our main source of information on these historical figures.

The treatment of Cicero is a typical example of Plutarch's method. First Plutarch gives us the life of Demosthenes, the greatest Greek orator. The life of Cicero follows, and then he offers a comparison of the two. He writes, for example, that "the power of persuading and governing the people did, indeed, equally belong to both, so that those who had armies and camps at command stood in need of their assistance; as Chares, Diopithes, and Leosthenes of Demosthenes', Pompey and young Caesar of Cicero's."

And yet Plutarch does not compare the substance of their speeches, except to say that in some cases Cicero seems too enamored of his own skill and that it is "an ignoble thing for any man to admire and relish the glory of his own eloquence." Instead, Plutarch focuses on the men's "natural dispositions . . . and their lives as statesmen." Much like the Shelf, in his treatment of Cicero, Plutarch passes over the very thing for which Cicero is most remembered.

In explaining this choice, Plutarch begins with what seems like an unrelated argument about the advantages of living in a big city. Because history must be "collected from materials gathered by observation and the reading of works not easy to be got in all places, nor written always in [one's] own language," it is particularly important for the historian "to reside in some city of good note, addicted to liberal arts, and populous." There, Plutarch writes, the historian "may have plenty of all sorts of books, and upon inquiry may hear and inform himself of such particulars as, having escaped the pens of writers, are more faithfully preserved in the memories of men, lest his work be deficient in many things, even those which it can least dispense with." But Plutarch himself lived not in a "city of good note" but in a small Greek town, and although he had traveled to Rome and other parts of Italy, he had had little time to learn the "Roman language." Therefore, he explains, "it was very late, and in the decline of my age, before I applied myself to the reading of Latin authors":

But to appreciate the graceful and ready pronunciation of the Roman tongue, to understand the various figures and connection of words, and such other ornaments, in which the beauty of speaking consists, is, I doubt not, an admirable and delightful accomplishment; but it requires a degree of practice and study which is not easy, and will better suit those who have more leisure, and time enough yet before them for the occupation.

It was a surprise to learn that Plutarch and I had much the same problem with Cicero. But Plutarch also saw a peculiar advantage in coming to Latin "in the decline of [his] age." When he finally did, he writes, "that which happened to me, may seem strange, though it be true; for it was not so much by the knowledge of words, that I came to the understanding of things, as by my experience of things I was enabled to follow the meaning of words." This is just how I felt as I recommitted myself to the Harvard Classics—that life was teaching me about these books just as much as the books were teaching me about life. My day with Peter at the Museum of Natural History did more for my understanding of both Darwin and Cicero than many pages of explication would have done.

At work in Plutarch's comparative method is not just the old truism that history can teach us about our moment, but the understanding that history is itself embedded in our moment, as our moment is embedded in whatever will come next. And it's not by the knowledge of words that I came to understand this thing, but by my experience of things that I came to follow his words. It is all here with us. The past is buried deep in the ground of the present; tomorrow is written above us, in the stars of today.

THE HARVARD CLASSICS

DRYDEN

April, or "Mambrino's Helmet"

When my twin brother Jim and I were young altar boys, the Easter Triduum—Holy Thursday, Good Friday, Easter Sunday—was the ultimate test. Christmas drew bigger crowds, but this was the weekend that really mattered: the birth meant little without the death and resurrection. Besides, Christmas Mass was just a normal Sunday liturgy, albeit with better music. But each service during Easter week had its unique elements—the washing of the feet, the veneration of the cross and the stripping of the altar, the procession of the paschal candle. It was as if we'd arrived after a long season at the Final Four, only to find that all the rules had been changed.

At some point early in the week leading up to the holy days, we would be excused from class at our elementary school, St. David's, to go across the street to the Church of Saint Thomas More, where Father Halborg would conduct a dry run through the three services. He was a stern, particular man, but prone to bursts of spontaneous, irreverent humor. Naturally, he wanted to get everything right, and Jim and I were never in any great hurry to get back to school, so we rehearsed with slow deliberation, and the sessions seemed to last all afternoon. Starting on Thursday, the services themselves were up to three hours long, and each required additional preparation for which we arrived early each day. By the time we were finished on Sunday afternoon, we felt as though we had spent the whole week in that church. Although we always had baskets and egg hunts and everything else that comes with the holiday, when I think of Easter I think of kneeling at the altar of Saint Thomas More with the smell of incense in my nose. I think of the little brass bell that had to be rung just right to make it sound out. (The trick was in the wrist, not the hand.) And I think of putting my shoulder to a large wooden cross while a line of strangers, neighbors, and friends waited to press their hands and lips against it.

I don't for a moment regret these memories. Altar service wasn't something we were pushed or even especially encouraged to do. We did it because we wanted to. There was a certain excitement to it. Waiting with the priests in the sacristy, peering out occasionally to watch the pews fill up, is probably the closest I'll ever come to being backstage on opening night. There was also a sense, which admittedly bordered at times on smugness, that one was a part of something significant—I'm tempted to say, something "adult," though by the time I became an adult myself I no longer felt its magic. Most of our friends at school were indifferent to religion, but this attitude was wholly alien to me. Faced with the imposing presence of faith in my family's life, I saw only two choices: stand consciously apart from it, as I do now; or allow myself to be swallowed up, as I did then.

In part because my brother and I always served the Sunday morning Mass on Easter, it was many years before I went to the Easter Vigil held on Saturday night. It may be the only Catholic ritual that I saw for the first time with adult eyes, the only one that had no childhood associations. I'd already given up my faith when I attended the vigil Mass for the first time; I'd already chosen to stand aside—so it's difficult to explain just how much that Mass moved me.

My family now attends Saint Ignatius Loyola, the Jesuit church around the corner from my old high school, which was also run by Jesuits. Saint Ignatius is large and beautiful in the old European manner. It has a boxy Gothic Revival street front on Park Avenue and a Renaissance-style basilica within. High above the altar, Jesus Christ sits enthroned beside two large palm trees (an odd, inscrutable touch that makes me think each time I enter of Wallace Stevens's poem about "the palm at the end of the mind"). The church also has one of the largest pipe organs in the world. But one forgets this on that Saturday evening each year, because the lights are turned off and the entire place goes dark.

Much of the meaning of the Catholic faith rests in its sense of tradition, a feeling of continuity with the past—it is the one thing I still hold on to. But this moment of darkness seems atavistic in a different way. Religious thinkers sometimes speak of the physical space of the church as a kind of portal between the profane and the sacred. For all my skepticism, this is how I feel in that moment. For a brief time, I'm returned to a world whose most unmistakable characteristic is its mystery. Even the shuffling of my family beside me suggests some inchoate, undiscoverable meaning.

Then there is a single light: in the center of the church, the priest lights the Easter fire and from it the paschal candle, a symbol of Christ's light on earth, which struggles to illuminate the enormous space. From this one candle are lit several smaller ones, held by altar boys and girls of about the age I was when so much of my life seemed to be given over to these ceremonies. They in turn light the candles of the parishioners sitting near them. The entire congregation has been given candles on the way into the church, and now the flame spreads out in all directions like a living thing expanding to fill the emptiness of the room.

All the while, the priest reads from his missal, reciting prayers that describe and supplement what we are all watching. But the moment always strikes me as entirely visual and fundamentally inexplicable. Although I'm trying my best to describe it now, it's not something that words can easily convey. Each candle in turn lights two or three, so that the progress of the flame quickens until it reaches a tipping point. Where there was mostly darkness there is all at once nothing but light. Though I don't believe in this faith and at times even feel anger toward it, I find myself in tears at that moment.

Part of me thinks it wrong to allow myself to enjoy the sublimity of a moment whose significance I can't ultimately accept. But for all we have learned in two thousand years, the world seems to me still basically mysterious, still dark, and for one night this flame seems like a beautiful way to answer that darkness.

For many reasons I was in a particularly receptive mood for the moment this year. One reason is that I had just finished reading the *Aeneid* (19 BCE). Virgil's poem occupies a strange place in literary history. It's not the first heroic epic; it draws quite consciously from the *Odyssey* and the *Iliad*. But whereas Homer is just a name attached to these two works, we know a great deal about Virgil and the circumstances in which he composed his poem. Virgil was born in northern Italy in the waning years of the Roman republic. We even know the date: October 15, 70 BCE. He was living in Rome at the time of Julius Caesar's assassination, and he was protected, throughout the civil war that followed, by the patronage of Octavius. When his patron was crowned Augustus, Virgil returned his favors by writing the *Aeneid*, which he composed quite consciously as the national epic of the new empire.

The poem tells the story of the founding of Rome by Aeneas after the Trojan War. That is to say, Virgil takes the same mythical moment that Homer, Aeschylus, and many other Greeks had already treated, but repurposes it. Like Aeschylus, Virgil uses the ancient past to speak about his own time. Since according to tradition Octavius's adoptive father Julius Caesar was a descendent of Aeneas, the story prefigures the founding of the new Rome after the civil war by the new Aeneas, Caesar Augustus. This is suggested quite early in the poem, in a speech made by Juno to Venus:

Thy son (nor is th' appointed season far)
In Italy shall wage successful war,
Shall tame fierce nations in the bloody field,
And sov'reign laws impose, and cities build,
Till, after ev'ry foe subdued, the sun
Thrice thro' the signs his annual race shall run:
This is his time prefix'd. Ascanius then,
Now call'd Iulus, shall begin his reign.
He thirty rolling years the crown shall wear,
Then from Lavinium shall the seat transfer,
And, with hard labor, Alba Longa build.
The throne with his succession shall be fill'd
Three hundred circuits more: then shall be seen
Ilia the fair, a priestess and a queen,
Who, full of Mars, in time, with kindly throes,

Shall at a birth two goodly boys disclose.
The royal babes a tawny wolf shall drain:
Then Romulus his grandsire's throne shall gain,
Of martial tow'rs the founder shall become,
The people Romans call, the city Rome. . . .
Then Caesar from the Julian stock shall rise,
Whose empire ocean, and whose fame the skies
Alone shall bound; whom, fraught with eastern spoils,
Our heav'n, the just reward of human toils,
Securely shall repay with rites divine;
And incense shall ascend before his sacred shrine.

In contrast, we know almost nothing about the composition of Virgil's Homeric models. Nor, for that matter, did Plato or Aeschylus, though they took those poems as their national epics. The poems seemed to have sprung from the ground. I suspect it would have been difficult for the Greeks to imagine a time when these epics didn't exist. They weren't just literature—they were history; they were religion and cosmology; they were ethics. They were in the air the Greeks breathed.

One of the many lessons that the Romans seem to have taken from the Greeks is that a culture, in order to be a culture, must tell itself a grand narrative, something larger than individual men and women. And when no such narrative existed, the culture needed to create one. In this sense, the appearance of Virgil—the only epic poet in history who might be fairly compared to Homer—at the very moment when a new culture was being born has about it a sense of fate, or perhaps design. Certainly Virgil himself seems to have thought of his career in this way.

In our own time, the grand narratives we tell ourselves might be historical or national, but they are most often religious. And that evening in the church, when light spread out to conquer darkness, contained within it the narrative that my family and millions of others have told. Participating in such a story is a communal act. But telling oneself out of it can only be done on an individual basis. This thought was part of what had me in tears as I stood in the half-light, waiting for the flame to arrive at the candle in my hand.

Though I know that the order of the Classics was mostly haphazard, it seemed a very sly move to follow the *Aeneid* with *Don Quixote* (1605), which I started reading for the fourth or fifth time that Easter Sunday. If it's generally considered the first "modern" novel, that is in part because it attempts to puncture these sorts of grand narratives. It's the first novel to register a change in the way we understand and relate to the world. It's an epic for a time in which the epic has become impossible. It's a romance novel, a novel of adventure, that mocks the romanticizing of adventure.

Miguel de Cervantes was himself no stranger to adventure by the time he wrote his masterpiece. He was born in 1547 and educated, as my brother and I were, by Jesuit priests. After traveling to Italy during his youth, Cervantes found work as a soldier. Perhaps he had elevated ideas of the glory this might bring him. Instead, he lost the use of one arm at the Battle of Lepanto in 1571. The battle was considered a landmark in the Spaniards' fight against the Moors, but now it's mostly known because of the wound Cervantes suffered there. He would later be captured by the Moors and imprisoned for some time in Algiers. It's said that he made several failed efforts at escape—efforts one is tempted now to call quixotic, as they were more likely to bring death than freedom. As it was, they brought neither. Upon being ransomed by his family and brought back to Spain, Cervantes began to write; because of his injury, he was no good for anything else. (This part of his life recalls Saint Ignatius Loyola, who came to religion after being badly wounded in the seige of Pamplona. In the church in New York that bears his name, this battle is depicted above the altar, beside Christ and those palm trees.)

Cervantes' writing career began with a pastoral poem that brought him little success. After this, he invented a character who so perfectly embodied the risks of telling oneself into a grand narrative that he became a permanent figure in western culture:

> There lived not long since, in a certain village of the Mancha, the name whereof I purposely omit, a gentleman of their calling that use to pile up in their halls old lances, halberds, morions, and such other armours and weapons. He was, besides, master of an ancient target, a lean stallion, and a swift greyhound. His pot consisted daily of somewhat more beef than mutton: a gallimaufry each night, collops and eggs on Saturdays, lentils on Fridays, and now and then a lean pigeon on Sundays, did consume three parts of his rents; the rest and remnant thereof was spent on a jerkin of fine puce, a pair of velvet hose, with pantofles of the same for the holy-days, and one suit of the finest vesture; for therewithal he honoured and set out his person on the workdays.

The man—his name may be Quixada or Quesada or more likely Quixana; no one is quite sure—becomes so consumed with reading novels of chivalry that he neglects his household and even sells off many acres of farmable land to buy more books. Satire is one of Cervantes' greatest strengths, and he has obvious fun describing and even quoting from some of the silly books that Quixana has been reading.

Now, I know from experience that once seated in his library with a stack of books a man of this sort is likely, by sheer force of inertia, to stay there. But Cervantes has faith in the power of books, for good or for ill, to send us back into world. What happens next is described so well by the author that one couldn't possibly resort to paraphrase:

In resolution, he plunged himself so deeply in his reading of these books, as he spent many times in the lecture of them whole days and nights; and in the end, through his little sleep and much reading, he dried up his brains in such sort as he lost wholly his judgment. His fantasy was filled with those things that he read, of enchantments, quarrels, battles, challenges, wounds, wooings, loves, tempests, and other impossible follies. . . . Finally, his wit being wholly extinguished, he fell into one of the strangest conceits that ever a madman stumbled on in this world; to wit, it seemed unto him very requisite and behooveful, as well for the augmentation of his honour as also for the benefit of the commonwealth, that he himself should become a knight-errant, and go throughout the world, with his horse and armour, to seek adventures, and practise in person all that he had read was used by knights of yore; revenging of all kinds of injuries, and offering himself to occasions and dangers, which, being once happily achieved, might gain him eternal renown.

As an aspiring novelist, I'd read *Don Quixote* several times in various translations by the time I came to these words that Easter Sunday, but never before had I identified so strongly with this man who has given his days and nights over to reading books until he becomes completely enchanted by them. *His fantasy was filled with those things that he read.*

Cervantes, ever the comedian, makes great sport of Quixana's preparations to go out into the world. Quixana finds a set of "old rusty arms" that had belonged to his great-grandfather and had long sat "forgotten in a by-corner of his house." He tries to fix them up, but finds that there is no helmet except a "plain morion," that is, the cheap, mass-produced helmet worn by foot soldiers. But the man is nothing if not resourceful, and "he by his industry supplied that want." Taking "certain papers," he pastes together a proper brim, or "beaver," for the helmet. Then he goes to test his handiwork: "He out with his sword and gave it a blow or two, and with the very first did quite undo his whole week's labour." So he begins again and this time, "without making a second trial," he declares himself happy with his work. In many ways this encapsulates the story of Quixana—wearing his great-grandfather's rusty arms, he makes himself a helmet from the pages of a book. He tests the helmet and, when it breaks, he satisfies himself by choosing not to test it a second time.

The next step is to give himself a name—Don Quixote de la Mancha—and find a lady—Dulcinea—in whose honor he may complete his acts of chivalry. His broken-down workhorse becomes the steed Rosinante. The only thing left is to find himself a squire.

Don Quixote dealt with a certain labourer, his neighbour, an honest man (if the title of honesty may be given to the poor), but one of a very shallow wit; in resolution, he said so much to him, and persuaded him so earnestly, and made him so large promises, as the poor fellow determined to go away with him, and serve him as his squire. Don Quixote, among many other things, bade him to dispose himself willingly to depart with him; for now and then such an adventure might present itself, that, in as short space as one would take up a couple of straws, an island might be won, and he be left as governor thereof. With these and such like promises, Sancho Panza (for so he was called) left his wife and children, and agreed to be his squire.

Sancho Panza has a clearer vision of the world, but unlike Don Quixote he doesn't trust what he sees. In his simplicity, Sancho assumes that he misunderstands Quixote's world, and he rarely doubts the vision that Quixote describes to him, no matter how little relation it bears to what presents itself in front of his own eyes.

Of the misadventures that follow, everyone knows the first: the famous battle with the windmills. That is, to Sancho Panza they are windmills, but to Don Quixote they are giants, and he charges them, getting knocked on his ass in the process. But running into windmills is after all a victimless crime, and it gives little sense of the destructiveness—to himself and to others— that Don Quixote's delusions will bring. He frees criminals working on a chain gang. He beats up strangers for no reason at all. He nearly kills himself and Sancho dozens of times. The book is rather cartoonish in its physical cruelty, going beyond Tom and Jerry to the point of Itchy and Scratchy. All the while Quixote believes himself to be having adventures of the most elevated kind.

At a certain point during Don Quixote's travels, something happens to the reader, and it seems that the same thing must have happened to Cervantes himself during the composition of the book. Despite all their absurd destructiveness and all their unintended consequences, Quixote's delusions come to seem dignified. It is as though the real fault rests in the world, which so stubbornly refuses to conform to Quixote's elevated vision. I imagine each reader arrives at this point at a different moment. For me, it begins with Mambrino's helmet.

Of course, the helmet doesn't really exist. It's another one of Quixote's fantasies. Not long into his adventures, Don Quixote finds his paper visor broken. At this point, in a moment of typically vague and confused grandeur, he vows "not to eat on table-cloth, nor sport with . . . wife, and other things, which, although I do not now remember, I give them here for expressed, until I take complete revenge on him that hath done me this outrage." Like all his vows, this one is compromised and eventually abandoned. The knight and his squire continue on their way, and it begins to rain.

> Don Quixote espied one a-horseback, that bore on his head somewhat that glistered like gold; and scarce had he seen him, when he turned to Sancho, and said, "Methinks, Sancho, that there's no proverb that is not true; for they are all sentences taken out of experience itself, which is the universal mother of sciences! and specially that proverb that says, 'Where one door is shut, another is opened.' I say this because, if fortune did shut yesternight the door that we searched, deceiving us in the adventure of the iron maces, it lays us now wide open the door that may address us to a better and more certain adventure, whereon, if I cannot make a good entry, the fall shall be mine, without being able to attribute it to the little knowledge of the fulling-maces, or the darkness of the night; which I affirm because, if I be not deceived, there comes one towards us that wears on his head the helmet of Mambrino, for which I made the oath."

THE HELMET OF MAMBRINO

What Don Quixote takes for the helmet of Mambrino is in fact a basin that this man, a barber who is on his way to let blood in the next town, has put on his head to protect himself from the rain. The barber "rode on a grey ass," Cervantes explains, "and that was the reason why Don Quixote took him to be a dapple-grey steed, a knight, and a helmet of gold; for he did, with all facility, apply everything which he saw to his raving chivalry and ill-errant thoughts." Don Quixote charges at the unsuspecting man, who drops the basin as he attempts to escape. He has given up Mambrino's helmet, which Don Quixote orders Sancho Panza to pick up and place on his master's head.

Sancho laughs at this request, but then he remembers Quixote's temper and stops himself. When Quixote asks why has was laughing he answers that he found it funny "to think on the great head the pagan owner of this helmet had; for it is for all the world like a barber's basin."

> "Know, Sancho, that I imagine," quoth Don Quixote, "that this famous piece of this enchanted helmet did fall, by some strange accident, into some one's hands that knew not the worth thereof, and seeing it was of pure gold, without knowing what he did, I think he hath molten the half, to profit himself therewithal, and made of the other half this, which seems a barber's basin, as thou sayst: but be it what it list, to me who knows well what it is, his transmutation makes no matter; for I will dress it in the first town where I shall find a smith, as that which the God of Forges made for the God of War shall not surpass, no, nor come near it; and in the meanwhile I will wear it as I may, for something is better than nothing."

It is here that my heart breaks for Don Quixote: *Something is better than nothing.* The rest of the book is punctuated by such moments, when Don Quixote is given glimpses of the benighted world beneath his fantasy. And thereby a new problem is presented. What are we to do with a world that gives us basins, when we want to live in a world of enchanted helmets?

At the end of the novel's second part (which isn't included in the Classics), Don Quixote gives up his grand idea of being a knight-errant and returns to his home. He even sells off all the books that had driven him to folly. We are no longer in the realm of satire and broad comedy; this disavowal can be seen only as tragic. In this way, Quixote becomes a template for later romance-sodden heroines such as Anna Karenina and Emma Bovary, who are also defeated by reality. His effort to live in a world of his own imagining isn't comic; it's heroic. And so, in the end, Cervantes's novel does become a kind of epic.

I still had Don Quixote's fate in mind the next week when I started reading the selection from *The Thousand and One Nights* (or the *Arabian Nights,* c. 900, translated 1706). This work had existed in various forms throughout the Eastern world for more than eight hundred years before it came to Europe in French and English translations. All the earlier versions share more or less the same framing device. King Shahryar is wronged by the woman he loves, and from then on he kills each of his wives at the end of their wedding night, until he marries Scheherazade, who captivates him with her storytelling. Because she ends each night in the middle of a story, the king must let her live so that he can hear the end of her tales. In the process, he falls in love with her and decides to spare her life. This is a perfect device for such a collection, allowing and even encouraging the nesting of one story within another, the buildup of suspense and complication of plot, and the insertion of new material at any point.

This book might be considered the first of the few non-Western works in the Shelf. But in fact its legacy is a bit more complex. Many of the stories we know best from the *Arabian Nights*—like Aladdin's lamp or Ali Baba and the forty thieves—weren't in any of the collections until they made their way to Europe in the early nineteenth century. (These stories, which are nonetheless real Middle Eastern tales, are included in an appendix to this volume.) One might argue that European translations of the *Arabian Nights* tell us less about the Orient than about Orientalism—that is, about the way the West has exoticized the East for its own purposes. At the very least, it must be understood that the inclusion of the work in the Harvard Classics has to do with its importance to nineteenth century European culture, not with any pioneering effort at multiculturalism.

What struck me most as I read these stories, some quite familiar and others entirely new, is that they all take place not in the world of the barber's basin but in the world of Mambrino's helmet. That is, the tales occupy a world of enchantment: of genies—or "efrits"—and magic. This world is not always, or even usually, good. In fact, most of the supernatural creatures are mischievous at best and malicious at worst. The one exception, of course, is Allah, who must be relied on for protection: like so many Western folk tales, the *Arabian Nights* attempts to reconcile monotheism with the existence of more local and limited spirits.

The first story that Scheherazade tells the king is "The Merchant and the Jinni." In it, a wealthy merchant travels to a neighboring country "to collect what was due to him." Along the way, he stops under a tree. While taking his rest, the merchant eats a date, throwing the pit aside.

Immediately there appeared before him an Efrit, of enormous height, who, holding a drawn sword in his hand, approached him, and said, Rise, that I may kill thee, as thou hast killed my son. The merchant asked him, How have I killed thy son? He answered, When thou atest the date, and threwest aside the stone, it struck my son upon the chest, and, as fate had decreed against him, he instantly died.

The merchant prays to Allah and asks the Jinni to spare him. Giving up on this, he asks at least to be allowed to settle up his accounts, and he promises to return in a year to accept his fate. He continues his journey, settles his accounts, and goes home to tell his family what happened. After this, "He appointed a guardian over his children, and remained with his family until the end of the year; when he took his grave-clothes under his arm, bade farewell to his household and neighbours, and all his relations, and went forth, in spite of himself; his family raising cries of lamentation, and shrieking."

When he arrives back at the tree where he'd sat to rest, the merchant meets with three sheiks who ask him why he is waiting there. He tells them about his encounter with the Jinni. Soon enough, the Jinni returns and prepares to take the merchant's life. At this point the first sheik intervenes and says, "O thou Jinni, and crown of the kings of the Jann, if I relate to thee the story of myself and this gazelle, and thou find it to be wonderful, and more so than the adventure of this merchant, wilt thou give up to me a third of thy claim to his blood?" The Jinni answers, "Yes, O sheykh; if thou relate to me the story, and I find it to be as

thou hast said, I will give up to thee a third of my claim to his
blood."

Each sheik in turn tells a story in exchange for a third of the
Jinni's blood-claim, and at the end they have earned the full share
and can set the merchant free. This tale is typical of the way stories proliferate in the *Nights*. It's also an example of the book's
wonderful parallelism. Just as Scheherazade herself suffers under
a death sentence from which she attempts to escape through
storytelling, so the characters in her stories are sentenced to
death—usually through no fault of their own—and must rely
on stories to save them. There is, then, a kind of desperation in
this proliferation of tales. These stories are no mere entertainments: they are the only thing keeping Scheherazade from the
void.

By the time that I finished Scheherazade's tales, Mimi wasn't getting out of bed very often, and we would take turns sitting beside her in the small guest room, which couldn't accommodate
more than two or three of us. One night while she lay in there
with her two sons beside her, Mimi asked for some music to be
played, perhaps as a distraction from her pain. I was standing in
the next room, and I came in when I heard her. Earlier in the
year, Jim, Alice, and I had given Mimi an iPod for her birthday,
and she often listened to it as she tried to get to sleep. She had a
preference for early Elvis (she kept a laughable but much-loved
picture of him in her apartment). In the process of setting up
her iPod, we'd downloaded a number of his songs, along with
some standard pop hits from the 1960s, onto the computer in
the guest room. And now, when she asked to listen to some
music, I clicked iTunes open. As I walked out, I closed the door

behind me, leaving her two sons to sit by her side while the Lovin' Spoonful sang "Do You Believe in Magic?"

Soon after that day, the doctors decided against further "active treatment" in Mimi's case. After hearing this, my cousin Paul put in a call to nearly every oncologist at every hospital in New York City. Each one broke his visor or knocked him off his horse, but still he got up and went at it again. Something was better than nothing.

My parents called a hospice nurse. The woman meant well, but we decided to send her home before her first session was through. We needed all the help we could find to make Mimi better, but if she wasn't going to get better then we needed to be with her. The family filled the apartment at all hours. Hardly an hour passed in any room, whether Mimi was in it or not, before someone took out rosary beads. And if Mimi was in the room, whoever brought out the beads would place them in her hands, the hands that had gone over the rosary every night for as long as I had known her.

And did I pray with them?

In truth, I didn't. But I stayed with them as they prayed, and I believed in their prayers, even if I couldn't voice any myself. I know what those prayers were, and so I know that they were not answered. There was a time when I might have thought that because none of this effort came to anything in the end, it therefore didn't matter. But I am working now in my way toward telling you this: more than anything, I wanted then—more than anything, I want now—to believe in Mambrino's helmet. I want nothing to do with the spectacle of an old man in his great-grandfather's rusty armor, running around with a basin on his head. I want to live in a world of monsters and heroic knights who defeat them.

May, or "To the Daughters of the Air!"

I didn't read much during the first half of May, which brought Mimi's last days. A hospital bed was ordered and moved into our library. My aunt Jaime's oldest daughter, Anne, who is a nurse, worked hard to keep Mimi comfortable and to give the rest of us some idea of what to expect.

After the funeral at Saint Ignatius Loyola, we drove in a procession out to Long Island, to the family plot, where we buried Mimi beside her husband, her parents, and Jaime's husband, Jack. Then we walked with heads bowed across the grass to the waiting motorcade to find that one of the drivers had locked his keys in the car.

"She was a saint," more than one acquaintance had told me that morning. In this case the remark had no trace of sentimental revisionism to it; this is very much how many people who knew Mimi thought of her while she was still alive. But when we found ourselves locked out of the car that was supposed to drive us to the reception, we felt the presence of the mischievous, irreverent Mimi—the side of her that I think those who loved her best loved best. We could almost hear her laughter at the sight of us standing there.

Near the end of the month, I started my reading again with the volume called "Folk-lore and Fable," the centerpiece of which is a collection of the Grimms' *Household Tales* (compiled c. 1815). These tales are a Western counterpart to the *Arabian Nights*—stories that have been around in one form or another for hundreds of years, and many of which, in some form, children still learn today. Like the *Nights,* they describe an enchanted and often dangerous world, but with fairies and goblins instead of jinnis and efrits.

It was a relief to turn to this volume. I knew that in my present emotional state I couldn't have managed Greek tragedy or German philosophy, but fairy tales seemed like just the escape I needed. My nieces, who were four and two at the time, loved nothing so much as Disney's princesses. I thought it a nice touch that all their favorites—Cinderella, Snow White, and the Little Mermaid Ariel—could be found in these pages.

A few weeks earlier, Alice's older daughter Holly had burst into my parents' apartment and announced, "We're having a baby!" My sister's pregnancy was one of the few things—along with the recent engagements of both my brother Jim and my cousin Michael —giving our family joy. Now, I felt as though I were being given permission to return to childhood for a few days.

The Grimms were librarians and philologists who set out at the beginning of the nineteenth century to preserve the folk-lore of their native culture. Most of the stories they collected were told to them by Prussian peasants, and they gave their

collection the title *Kinder- und Hausmärchen*: children's and household tales. Indeed, these stories can be seen as the domestic
equivalent of the more public heroic legends. (One of the
Grimm brothers wrote a book about German heroic legends.)
Like the earliest bardic epics, these tales were transmitted orally
for generations before they were ever written down; their "author" is the culture itself. And if societies as a whole need grand
heroic narratives, we seem, on the individual level, to need
these more domestic stories.

To some degree, I understood this before I started reading the
"household tales," and I knew as we all do that many fairy tales
are in fact rather dark and disorienting. So I don't know why I per-
sisted in thinking of this volume as a childish indulgence. Perhaps
it was something I needed to tell myself just to get reading again.
At any rate, I quickly understood that these tales offered something quite different from escape. Even a cursory look at their
titles—"Rapunzel," "Hansel and Gretel," "Rumpelstiltskin"—
reveals how many of these stories still hold a place in our cultural
consciousness, but I was most profoundly moved by one that I'd
never known before in any form. It's called "Our Lady's Child,"
and it begins in this way:

> Hard by a great forest dwelt a wood-cutter with his wife, who
> had an only child, a little girl of three years old. They were,
> however, so poor that they no longer had daily bread, and did
> not know how to get food for her. One morning the wood-
> cutter went out sorrowfully to his work in the forest, and while
> he was cutting wood, suddenly there stood before him a tall
> and beautiful woman with a crown of shining stars on her head,
> who said to him, "I am the Virgin Mary, mother of the child
> Jesus. Thou art poor and needy, bring thy child to me, I will

take her with me to be her mother, and care for her." The wood-cutter obeyed, brought his child, and gave her to the Virgin Mary, who took her up to heaven with her.

The child lives happily in heaven until she is fourteen years old, when the Virgin Mary goes on a long journey and leaves her "the keys to the thirteen doors of heaven." She is permitted to open twelve of these doors, but the thirteenth is forbidden. Naturally, she gives in to temptation and opens the thirteenth door. She finds within "the Trinity sitting in fire and splendour." She touches the light they give off, which turns her finger gold. When the Virgin returns from her journey, she asks the girl three times if she has opened the thirteenth door, and three times the girl denies it—at which point, she's banished from heaven.

First she falls into a deep sleep. When she wakes up, she is back on earth, "in the midst of a wilderness." She tries to cry out for help, but she finds that she can't make any sound. Next, she tries to run away, but "whithersoever she turned herself, she was continually held back by thick hedges of thorns through which she could not break." There is in this wilderness an old hollow tree, into which the girl climbs to spend the night. She continues to sleep in this tree for many years, surviving on wild berries and fallen nuts. Her clothes become torn, and in the winter she must wrap herself in fallen leaves to keep from freezing to death. In this way, "she found a shelter from storm and rain, but it was a miserable life, and bitterly did she weep when she remembered how happy she has been in heaven, and how the angels had played with her." When the winter ends and the sun returns, she sits in front of the tree with only her long hair covering her: "Thus she sat year after year, and felt the pain and misery of the world."

But the young girl's fall from heaven is only the beginning of the story. One day, while she sits feeling the pain and misery of the world, a young king approaches her. He falls in love with her, and they marry, though she still can't speak. He takes her to his castle, where she eventually bears him a child. The Virgin then reappears, asking her to admit that she opened the forbidden thirteenth door. She's allowed to speak only long enough to repeat her denial, at which point the Virgin takes her child from her and leaves her once again speechless. This pattern is repeated twice.

After the disappearance of three children, the king's subjects come to believe that their queen has been eating her babies. They put her on trial, and because she can't speak, she's unable to defend herself. The people sentence her to be burned alive. They gather wood together and bind her to the stake. But as "the fire began to burn round about her, the hard ice of pride melted, her heart was moved by repentance." She wishes she were able to confess before her death that she opened the door. In that moment, her voice returns to her, and she calls out, "Yes, Mary, I did it."

As soon as she makes her confession, a rain comes to extinguish the flames. Then the Virgin Mary descends from heaven with the woman's two sons beside her and the newborn daughter in her arms. "He who repents his sin and acknowledges it," Mary tells her, "is forgiven." Then she returns the three children, gives the mother back her speech, and grants her "happiness for her whole life."

I've read this story many times since that May (the whole thing is just four pages long), and I still don't know quite what to make of it. It has an ostensibly happy ending, and a standard fairy-tale moral: "He who repents his sin and acknowledges it, is forgiven." But these aren't the elements that strike me each time I read "Our Lady's Child."

First of all, there are the girl's parents, the woodcutter and his wife, too poor to feed their child. This circumstance recurs many times in the Grimms' tales; for instance, the same need forces Hansel and Gretel's father to leave them to starve in the forest. Whereas the heroic legends take place on the battlefield and in banquet halls, these stories take place in the woods, and the great battle is for subsistence. It seems to me that a truly happy ending would reunite the girl with her parents, but there's no suggestion that such a thing is possible in this world.

I think of the girl, waking up alone in the wilderness, hedged in on every side, unable even to cry out. *Thus she sat year after year, and felt the pain and misery of the world.* And then I understand her stubborn unwillingness to admit her transgression. Those doors, like the tree of knowledge in the Garden of Eden, seem like a trap that has been set for her. Her obstinacy in the face of this trap strikes me as one of the story's most hopeful aspects, and I read her final admission as a defeat for which being "granted her happiness" is a small recompense. The very phrasing—"granted her happiness"—confirms that happiness is not something to be gained on one's own terms but is offered or withheld by the world as it sees fit. This conclusion is underscored by the fact that her "forbidden fruit" has been nothing less than direct access to God.

As I read the more familiar tales in this collection, I often found the same thing to be true. Life in these stories is full of hardship, and no final reward can undo this fact. "Cinderella" begins with merciless abruptness:

The wife of a rich man fell sick, and as she felt that her end was drawing near, she called her only daughter to her bedside and said, "Dear child, be good and pious, and then the good God will always protect thee, and I will look down on thee from heaven and be near thee." Thereupon she closed her eyes and departed.

Each day after this, the daughter went to her mother's grave to weep. She did so even as the winter came on and "the snow spread a white sheet over the grave." By the time the spring came and the snow melted, her father had taken a new wife: "The woman had brought two daughters into the house with her, who were beautiful and fair of face, but vile and black of heart. Now began a bad time for the poor step-child."

There is something very moving in this matter-of-fact last sentence. It reminded me of the passing remark, "but it was a miserable life," in "Our Lady's Child." Such bad times come as no great surprise in this world. And there is nothing fanciful or cartoonish about the stepfamily's treatment of Cinderella. They steal her clothes and her sheets, refuse her a place at the table, make her do all the housework, and do her "every imaginable injury."

When her father goes into town, the stepsisters ask him to bring them back dresses, but Cinderella only wants the first branch that knocks against his hat on the way home. An odd request, and not just because of its modesty. He brings her a hazel branch, which she plants at her mother's grave. Cinderella's tears water the branch until it grows into a "handsome tree." Three times a day, Cinderella sits beneath the tree, weeping and praying. When she does, "a little white bird always came on the tree, and if Cinderella expressed a wish, the bird threw down to her what she had wished for." This detail is expressed in the same simple tone as all of the girl's suffering.

Of course, in the more familiar version of this story, the tree and the bird are replaced by the fairy godmother, who is the

simple personification of wish fulfillment. But this development—the branch growing into a tree and the tree inviting the
arrival of the bird—is considerably more complex, and more
interesting. The modern alteration obscures the unavoidable
lesson of this story: it's not enough to wish for things; we must
pay for our happiness in tears shed at the graves of those we
love.

Time and again I found that these stories differed in important ways from the ones I had learned as a child. Each tale revealed itself as darker, stranger, and sadder than I had previously
known it to be. The tales the Grimms collected weren't at all
childlike escapism. But that made them far more meaningful
to me. I mentioned this to my mother, and she said that the
Cinderella she remembered was the Cinderella of the hazel branch
and the little bird. I wondered if my grandmother had read these
stories to my mother and my aunts out of the very volume I was
reading. It seemed like a great loss that the corrupted versions
should have come to overshadow these earlier ones.

In fairness to the fairy godmother and to dwarfs with names
like Sleepy and Sneezy, it may be that a work of popular imagination can't ever really be "corrupted." There is no definitive version of Cinderella or Snow White: each culture creates the one
it needs. There were doubtless many more versions that the
Grimms never found, tales that have since been lost. But the
matter of corruption is far more straightforward in the case of
Hans Christian Andersen, whose *Tales* (1835) follow the Grimms
in this volume. Andersen's work stands in relation to that of the
Grimms much as the *Aeneid* does to its Homeric predecessors.
They are the consciously literary efforts of a single author to
replicate what had once grown out of the collective. And, like
Virgil, Andersen succeeds remarkably in this effort.

The best of these tales, "The Little Mermaid" (or "Little Sea-Maid," as my translation has it) tells the story of the world beneath the water, where, "in the deepest spot of all," there is a Sea-Castle. The Sea-King is a widower—always in such stories the mother is lost—with six beautiful daughters. They know of the world above the water from the occasional drowned sailor who descends to their castle. Each sea princess, as she passes the age of fifteen, travels up to the surface, where she sits on the rocks to catch glimpses of the earth world. "What happens to those humans who don't drown?" asks the youngest princess. "Do they otherwise live forever above the water?"

Her grandmother explains that humans, too, must die. In fact, they have much shorter lives than the sea creatures, who all live to be three hundred years old. But sea creatures turn, at their death, into foam, without "even a grave down here among those we love." They are like the seaweed, she says, "which, when once cut through, can never bloom again." Humans, on the other hand, have immortal souls that live on after the death of their bodies. "As we rise up out of the waters and behold all the lands of the earth," she concludes, "so they rise up to unknown glorious places which we can never see."

When she hears about these souls, the Sea-maid tells her grandmother that she would give up all the years she has to live for just one day as a human with "a hope of partaking the heavenly kingdom."

"You must not think of that," her grandmother answers. "We feel ourselves far more happy and far better than mankind yonder." But the Sea-maid is insistent. Isn't there anything she can do, she asks, to win an immortal soul? Her grandmother explains the one way: "Only if a man were to love you so that you should be more to him than father or mother; if he should cling to you

with his every thought and with all his love." In such a circumstance, this man's soul would be imparted to her, even as he
would retain it for himself. But for a human to fall in love with
Sea-maid would be impossible, because the fish tail—considered
so beautiful in the water—is looked on as ugly on earth: "They
don't understand it; there one must have the clumsy supports
which they call legs, to be called beautiful."

As with so many of the Grimms' tales, most of the story that
follows is familiar. The mermaid Ariel falls in love with a prince
from the earth and strikes a deal with a sea witch who transforms
her tail into legs. Once changed, she can never turn back, and
she will perish as sea foam if the prince marries another. In the
movie version that my nieces loved, the mermaid marries the
prince, but Andersen's prince marries someone else, and Ariel's
only chance to save herself is to kill him, which she refuses to
do. There follows a passage that seems to me almost impossibly beautiful.

Now the sun rose up out of the sea. The rays fell mild and
warm upon the cold sea-foam, and the little Sea-maid felt
nothing of death. She saw the bright sun, and over her head
sailed hundreds of glorious ethereal beings—she could see
them through the white sails of the ship and the red clouds
of the sky; their speech was melody, but of such a spiritual
kind that no human ear could hear it, just as no human eye
could see them; without wings they floated through the air.
The little Sea-maid found that she had a frame like these, and
was rising more and more out of the foam.

"Whither am I going?" she asked; and her voice sounded like
that of other beings, so spiritual, that no earthly music could
be compared to it.

"To the daughters of the air!" replied the others. "A sea-maid has no immortal soul, and can never gain one, except she win the love of a mortal. Her eternal existence depends upon the power of another. The daughters of the air have likewise no immortal soul, but they can make themselves one through good deeds. . . . You, poor little Sea-maid, have striven with your whole heart after the goal we pursue; you have suffered and endured; you have by good works raised yourself to the world of spirits, and can gain an immortal soul after three hundred years."

And the little Sea-maid lifted her glorified eyes toward God's sun, and for the first time she felt them fill with tears. On the ship there was again life and noise. She saw the Prince and his bride searching for her; then they looked mournfully at the pearly foam, as if they knew that she had thrown herself into the waves. Invisible, she kissed the forehead of the bride, fanned the Prince, and mounted with the other children of the air on the rosy cloud which floated through the ether. After three hundred years we shall thus float into Paradise!

At the end of the month, my mother and I went out to the family house in Sag Harbor. It was strange being there without Mimi. In the twenty years since my grandmother's death, Mimi had become the matriarch of that house. As a schoolteacher with summers off, she stayed there for weeks at a time, usually painting. Sometimes she worked on jobs commissioned by friends. Otherwise she stripped and refinished furniture she found at yard sales and thrift shops. My mother had also been a schoolteacher, and the two of them spent many summer weeks together, while the rest of our families came out on weekends. If being there without Mimi was difficult for me, I could only imagine what it felt like for my mother. I tried my best that week to comfort and distract her. But after some time, I understood that she didn't want to be comforted or distracted. She wanted to be allowed to miss her sister. She wanted to take time to be sad.

While we were there, I read the next volume of the Classics, "Modern English Drama." The collection begins with Dryden's *All for Love* (1677), one of the high points of Restoration drama.

During Cromwell's rule, the Puritans closed the theaters in London, and public performances were banned. After the Restoration in 1660, when Charles II lifted this ban, the theater once again became the chief means of popular entertainment, as it continued to be for more than two hundred years. The earlier plays in this volume, from Dryden's retelling of the story of Antony and Cleopatra to eighteenth-century comedies by Richard Sheridan and Oliver Goldsmith, are clearly written in this spirit. They're spectacles with a crowded stage and quick-fire dialogue, meant above all to entertain. And they *are* entertaining, though not wholly satisfying on the page. When you are reading them, it helps to imagine a performance, to imagine the audience around you, responding like a sitcom laugh track to the witty barbs and cases of mistaken identity.

But the volume closes in the romantic era, with several so-called "closet dramas"—that is, plays meant to be read rather than staged. The achievement of these works is more poetic than dramatic, and in fact their authors—Shelley, Browning, and Byron—are known as poets rather than playwrights. Compared with the other plays in the volume, these plays have quite the opposite effect. Rather than encouraging one to imagine a charmed, raucous audience, bringing out the social aspects of the work, they seemed designed to emphasize solitude. The best of them, in fact, takes self-sufficiency as its subject.

Byron's *Manfred* (1817) begins with its title character alone, at midnight, in what the minimal stage directions describe as a "Gothic Gallery" in the Alps. He is tortured by some unnamed guilt. The exact nature of the problem is unclear; we only know that it will give him no peace, as he explains in an opening soliloquy.

> Sorrow is knowledge: they who know the most
> Must mourn the deepest o'er the fatal truth,
> The Tree of Knowledge is not that of Life.

As Manfred concludes his speech, he conjures seven spirits, which offer to give him whatever he wishes. He asks first for forgetfulness, then for self-oblivion. But the spirits, who are ageless and immortal, can give him only "that which [they] possess": "Kingdom, and sway, and strength, and length of days." These worldly goods hold nothing for Manfred. The one thing he wants—some release from his sorrowful knowledge—can't be provided by the spirit world, which "hath no power upon the past." The obvious solution is suicide, but there is some power that stops Manfred from taking his life and "makes it [his] fatality to live." He's stuck in what he believes to be the great predicament of man—"Half dust, half deity, alike unfit / To sink or soar."

Throughout the rest of the play, Manfred wanders through the alpine landscape surrounding his Gothic Gallery, seeking peace. He meets a hunter who seems to represent the unselfconscious man, as well as several more supernatural powers, including the "Witch of the Alps." He explains to this witch the nature of the knowledge that has troubled him so much. Throughout his life, he says, his "spirit walk'd not with the souls of men / Nor look'd upon the earth with human eyes." He held himself apart from others, preferring to spend his days alone in the wilderness. Eventually this life of solitude led him to the study of death:

> And then I dived,
> In my lone wanderings, to the caves of death,
> Searching its cause in its effect; and drew
> From wither'd bones, and skulls, and heap'd up dust,
> Conclusions most forbidden . . . I made
> Mine eyes familiar with Eternity.

The witch forces Manfred to admit that he wasn't really alone in this quest. He had a like-minded sister, Astarte. "She had the same lone thoughts and wanderings," he says. "The quest of hidden knowledge, and a mind / To comprehend the universe." Astarte is the source of Manfred's guilt: "I loved her, and destroy'd her!"

There has been much speculation about the nature of Manfred's transgression, especially because the play was written at about the time when Byron was accused of an incestuous relationship with his own sister. All we know is that after Astarte's death, Manfred is tortured by the knowledge he now possesses, and he hopes for the peace that only death can give him. As he tells the witch:

> Daughter of Air! I tell thee, since that hour—
> . . . Forgetfulness
> I sought in all, save where 't is to be found,
> And that I have to learn—my sciences,
> My long pursued and superhuman art,
> Is mortal here; I dwell in my despair—
>   And live—and live for ever.

The Witch of the Alps is a "daughter of the air" very different from the ones to whom the Sea-maid floats upon her death, but Manfred's dilemma isn't so different from hers. They are trapped between two worlds, one above and one below. Like the young girl peeking behind the thirteenth door, they have had a glimpse of something terrible in its power, something that is now being denied to them. They are separated from the people they love most. In recompense, they are offered life—three hundred years. But life with the new knowledge they hold becomes a torture to them. Just as Andersen's tale ends with the Sea-maid floating off to the daughters of the air, Byron's play ends with Manfred's release into death. With his last breath, he speaks to the abbot of a nearby monastery, who has expelled the spirits that surround Manfred.

"Old man!" he tells the abbot, "'tis not so difficult to die."

THE HARVARD CLASSICS

VERITAS

GOETHE

June, or "No Wiser Than Before"

In June my hives returned, red and swollen to diameters of several inches, covering my entire body but concentrated mostly around my head and feet. This might not have troubled me so much had I not been reading just then about the plague.

Several years ago, while I was still in graduate school, I lived in a tiny studio apartment in the SoHo neighborhood of Manhattan. One morning during my first summer there, I woke to find my skin dotted with what looked like insect bites. They were small discolorations, surrounded by quarter-size areas of swelling. It was a hot summer and I had no air conditioner, so I usually slept with the windows open. There were rips in the window screens that I'd covered with duct tape, but the tape sometimes fell off during the night, so I assumed that some bugs had found their way into my apartment and tucked in while I slept. Despite a fair amount of discomfort and scratching throughout the day, I didn't think much more about the apparent bites.

But I couldn't sleep the next night. I was hardly in bed before the itching started. It felt as if hundreds of little creatures were crawling over my body. Several times I leaped from bed and flicked on the lights, hoping to catch them scurrying for cover. But there was nothing. I ran my hands over my sheets and blanket. Still nothing. I turned off the lights and got back into bed, where the itching promptly started up again. I would have thought I was being paranoid, except that by the end of that sleepless night what had begun as perhaps a dozen bites was now a full-blown rash covering most of my body.

At that time, my cancer hadn't been in remission for long, and it took little more than a runny nose to send me in a panic to my oncologist's office. On this occasion I was there within the day. He examined me, drew some blood, and told me to take Benedryl. A few days later he called to confirm that there was nothing seriously wrong.

There was much talk going around about a bedbug infestation in Manhattan. But I had been assured that bedbugs were visible to the naked eye, and my subsequent dashes to the light switch to surprise these creatures were no more fruitful than the first. Still, I made a call to an exterminator. Then I set off several store-bought bug bombs. I threw out my sheets and blankets. I threw out a second set of same. Threw out my mattress and my bedspring. None of this made any difference. It became increasingly difficult to ignore the possibility that I was going insane.

Over the next months, I spent many nights on my hardwood floor. First I tried sleeping on my couch, which wasn't a couch exactly but a dorm room holdover that the good people at La-Z-Boy called a "chair-and-a-half," meaning that it was roughly half as wide as I am tall. In normal situations the chair-and-a-half converts into a bed. When you live in a studio on Thompson Street that rents for one thousand dollars a month, however, you can have bookcases on your walls or room to pull out your chair-and-a-half, but you can't have both. I could drape my legs

over the armrest, but they invariably came into contact with the
bed, and I would spend the night convinced that I was going to
wake up to find an extra toe on one of my feet. Thus, the hardwood floor.

In the end the problem just stopped when the weather turned
cool. The outbreaks returned each summer after that, though
never as severely, following me from apartment to apartment
and on trips out of New York, as though I were carrying an infestation around with me.

This summer the outbreak came on worse than ever before,
especially around my head and feet. Ever since I finished chemotherapy, I've shaved my head about once a week, and now
the swelling made my skull badly misshapen. Also, I walked
around all day pawing at my scalp, leaving casual observers to
wonder if someone without any hair could get head lice. And
then I started to worry about the plague.

Alessandro Manzoni's *The Betrothed* (the Five-Foot Shelf retains
its original Italian title, *I Promessi Sposi*) was written in 1825, but
it takes place during the seventeenth-century Spanish occupation of northern Italy, alluding throughout to the nineteenth-
century struggle for Italian unification and independence. It tells
the story of two young peasants: Renzo and Lucia. They are
engaged, but their love is thwarted by an evil Spanish aristocrat,
Don Rodrigo. The lovers are sent separately into hiding and must
find their way back to each other. The novel is part historical
romance in the style of Walter Scott and part ironic political
romance in the style of Stendhal, but the finest passages, at once
the most moving and the most gripping, come with the arrival

of the plague to Milan in 1630. "Sickness and deaths began rapidly to multiply," Manzoni writes, "with the unusual accompaniments of spasms, palpitation, lethargy, delirium, and those fatal symptoms, livid spots and sores; and these deaths were, for the most part, rapid, violent, and not unfrequently sudden, without any previous tokens of illness." As I read these words, I scratched at the spots on my temple and wondered what exactly qualified as "lethargy."

At first, most physicians were unwilling to admit that the plague was present, and those who contradicted them were said to be inciting the public. But eventually the truth became unavoidable. At its height, Manzoni writes, the death toll reached twelve hundred to fifteen hundred a day, and tens of thousands of victims were confined in quarantine centers called lazarettos. Several startling scenes are set in one of these lazarettos, part triage ward and part charnel house.

The novel's hero, Renzo, falls ill, but he recovers, and his brief brush with the illness leaves him immune. After Don Rodrigo, the evil aristocrat, dies of the plague, Renzo returns to his hometown looking for Lucia. He finds the place devastated. The few suffering survivors are unrecognizable.

Those like Renzo, who have recovered, become like a "privileged class," Manzoni writes, and those who haven't yet been infected live "in constant apprehension of it. They walked cautiously and warily about, with measured steps, gloomy looks, and haste at once and hesitation: for everything might be a weapon against them to inflict a mortal wound."

Of course, I understood that I probably didn't have a case of the bubonic plague. Yet during those sleepless nights, as I rolled around uncomfortably in bed, dreaming in sheer exhaustion but somehow still fully awake, I couldn't be quite sure. During the day, with my wits about me, I thought mostly of Renzo, the survivor among the dead.

When my twin brother, Jim, and I were freshmen in college, a car hit Jim near the campus. On the first night in the emergency room, a doctor told our family that he was unlikely to live until the morning. But he did. He spent the next two weeks unconscious, on a respirator, and his full recovery took more than a year. I've often thought it strange that identical twins should each come, at a young age but under entirely different circumstances, within kissing distance of death. It's even stranger, I suppose, that we both survived. I haven't spoken about these events very much with my brother, but I know that he found my illness more frightening than his accident, just as I found his accident more frightening than my illness. Not that each of us wasn't scared by his own emergency. I, at least, was terrified. But for both of us, the greater fear was being the one left behind.

As difficult as it is to watch someone you love in pain, to watch her body fail, to watch the countless minor and major indignities of dying that I haven't recorded here, it's even more difficult to go on without her. While Mimi was sick, we thought: if only we can make it through this. But once she was gone, we wanted only to return to the time when she was sick but still with us. Like Manfred or the Sea-maid, we were given one consolation: that we were still alive. But now our life felt empty.

Everywhere I looked, something reminded me of Mimi. I left my room each morning and walked down the hall that she had struggled to conquer with the help of her physical therapist. When I checked my e-mail, I sat at the computer in the guest room where Mimi had slept. As I read the Classics in the library,

my eyes wandered from the page to the spot in the room where
she used to park her wheelchair for much of the day.

I thought a lot about a line I'd read early in the year, from the
second volume of the Classics. At the end of Plato's *Apology*,
Socrates stands before his Athenian accusers after they have sentenced him to be poisoned. He speculates briefly on what may
await him but finally admits that it's impossible to say. Then, in
typically curt elegance, he concludes: "The hour of departure
has arrived, and we go our ways—I to die, and you to live. Which
is better, God only knows."

This epistemological humility is the signature Socratic note.
Earlier in the *Apology*, Socrates explains how he came to his reputation for wisdom ("That evil name," he calls it.) It seems that a
friend, Chaerephon, asked the oracle of Delphi whether any man
was wiser than Socrates, and the oracle answered no. "When I
heard the answer," Socrates continues, "I said to myself, What can
the god mean? and what is the interpretation of this riddle? for I
know that I have no wisdom, small or great."

In response to this "riddle," Socrates sets out to find a man
wiser than he. But when he questions a man known for his wisdom, Socrates is disappointed and concludes, "Well, although I
do not suppose that either of us knows anything really beautiful and good, I am better off than he is—for he knows nothing,
and thinks that he knows. I neither know nor think that I know.
In this latter particular, then, I seem to have slightly the advantage of him."

Socrates is one of the world's great ironists, so it's difficult to
say exactly how we are meant to take his insistence on his own
ignorance, which often implies the impossibility of any real knowledge. In reality, there are all sorts of things that people can know
with a fair degree of certainty. For example, we know that Plato

studied under Socrates and that he wrote the dialogues by which
Socrates' teaching comes down to us. But seen through the lens
of this closing remark—"Which is better, God only knows"—
Socrates' stance on knowledge is clarified: Though we can know
all sorts of things, the true value of this commonly available
knowledge is doubtful. Our most pressing questions—Why must
we die? What is death really like? How are we to live in the face of
death?—can never be answered. One mark of wisdom, then, may
be the ability to accept this limit to our knowledge.

But easier said than done. When I considered Socrates, reading the Classics was leading me to the troubling conclusion that
a great deal of what has been taken throughout history for
learning has in fact been a series of speculative forays beyond
the limits of the knowable. What's more, the writers and thinkers conducting these forays seem as aware of this fact as anyone. Strikingly, many of the best plays and poems in the Shelf
dramatize the human struggle for knowledge beyond our grasp,
the human unwillingness to accept natural limits. Thus, in *Paradise Lost* (and, of course, in its biblical source) we find Adam and
Eve expelled from the garden for eating from the tree of knowledge. The temptation of this fruit is wonderfully rendered by
Milton. When Eve tells the serpent that she will die if she eats
from the tree, he assures her she won't. (In fact, he's right, for
the short term at least.) He continues:

> Why, then, was this forbid? Why but to awe,
> Why but to keep ye low and ignorant,
> His worshipers? He knows that in the day
> Ye eat thereof your eyes, that seem so clear,
> Yet are but dim, shall perfectly be then
> Opened and cleared, and ye shall be as Gods.

"Your eyes, that seem so clear, yet are but dim." As soon as we hear these words, we recognize their truth. How tempting, then, to believe what follows: that our dim eyes may be made open and clear. In Milton's world, the human sin that results from this hope is redeemed by Jesus. In *Paradise Regained*, the Devil tempts Jesus in the desert with the prospect of worldly knowledge. "He who receives Light from above," Jesus replies, "no other doctrine needs." This rebuff comes in the last book of the poem, and it represents an undoing of Adam and Eve's decision to eat the fruit.

In such a scheme, a quest for too much knowledge is not just misguided but sinful, even blasphemous, like opening the thirteenth door expressly forbidden to us. Persisting in such a quest ultimately implies allegiance to the Devil. And yet it's an almost overwhelming temptation, one that only a few special figures in history—Socrates, Jesus—can resist. The seeker punished for pursuing knowledge beyond his grasp appears repeatedly in the Classics, and is exemplified in the figure of Faust.

The legend of Faust is said to have historical roots in a medieval German philosopher who claimed to practice magic and tell fortunes. He was publicly condemned by Martin Luther, among others. After his death in the 1540s, a rumor spread that he had received his powers in a pact with the Devil, who had taken his life in return. A version of Faust's story was published in German in 1587, and made its way in translation to England. This translation formed the basis for Christopher Marlowe's play *Dr. Faustus*, first performed around 1590. Marlowe had a fascination with men who attempt to attain the unattainable, so his play about Faust emphasizes the idea that Faust entered into league with the Devil in order to acquire knowledge beyond human capacity.

After Marlowe's play was written, Faust became a popular figure in puppet shows, and in this form he was repatriated to Germany and came to be taken up as a subject by the greatest of German poets, Goethe. Goethe's Faust is an altogether more complex figure than Marlowe's. But he begins in the same place, frustrated because all his years of study have brought him no real wisdom:

> I have, alas! Philosophy,
> Medicine, Jurisprudence too,
> And to my cost Theology,
> With ardent labour, studied through.
> And here I stand, with all my lore,
> Poor fool, no wiser than before.

The one lesson Faust's studies have taught him is "that we in truth can nothing know." He has come to the Socratic conclusion that knowledge is illusory, that it doesn't give us wisdom. But he also comes to a further conclusion: that all his studying has given him neither happiness nor power in the world nor control over the things that matter to him. "No dog in such fashion would longer live!" he declares. So he gives up the pursuit of worldly knowledge and gives himself over to magic—"In hope, through spirit-voice and might, / Secrets now veiled to bring to light." He conjures up a series of spirits, leading to the arrival in his study of the Devil's representative, Mephistopheles, "in the dress of a traveling scholar." Mephistopheles offers to serve Faust in every way in exchange for his soul, to be taken upon Faust's achieving a moment of perfect happiness. Faust accepts the offer:

> Be not afraid that I shall break my word!
> The scope of all my energy

Is in exact accordance with my vow . . .
Rent is the web of thought; my mind
Doth knowledge loathe of every kind.
In depths of sensual pleasure drown'd,
Let us our fiery passions still!

The vow will lead to tragedy by the end of the first part of
the poem, and Faust will wish that he'd never been born. Goethe,
however, does not side with Socrates, who concluded that we
should abandon the pursuit of the unknown. On the contrary,
Faust is redeemed in the second part of the poem, and this re-
demption comes largely by way of his persistent struggle.

Reading this poem so soon after Byron's *Manfred*, which takes
up many of the same themes, I thought about what had impelled
me to read the Classics in the first place. If it had been a simple
matter of acquiring knowledge, there would have been any number of better methods. After all, the Shelf excludes the last hundred years, and so it excludes a substantial portion of what we
now know about the world. (This point becomes painfully obvious when we read a work like *On the Origin of Species*, ground-
breaking in its day yet lacking in much information now widely
available.) Did I hope my reading would give me wisdom—that
elusive thing so easily confused with knowledge?

I don't think I approached the project with anything so grandly
ambitious in mind. But back in Sag Harbor, I looked over my
grandmother's shelves, where I had first found these volumes.
I remembered that I had started reading them with the idea that
they might bring me closer to her. Perhaps this is the knowledge
we are always after, though it's destined to remain out of reach:
the knowledge of those we have lost.

★   ★   ★

Where are our dead? How can we visit them? Must they really be lost to us? If there is anything truly unknowable, it would seem to be this. And yet a substantial portion of the Shelf is set in the land of the dead. In *The Frogs*, Aristophanes sends Dionysus to Hades to retrieve Euripides and save Greek drama. Later, Virgil sends Aeneas there to speak with his father. And then Virgil himself serves as Dante's guide in the *Inferno* (c. 1310), which initiates the greatest of all visits to the dead.

Dante's Pilgrim begins *The Divine Comedy* just as Goethe's Faust begins his poem: lost.

In the midway of this our mortal life,
I found me in a gloomy wood, astray
Gone from the path direct: and e'en to tell,
It were no easy task, how savage wild
That forest, how robust and rough its growth,
Which to remember only, my dismay
Renews, in bitterness not far from death.

While wandering through the gloomy wood in this state, he finds a man "whose voice seem'd faint with the long disuse of speech." "At Rome my life was past," the man explains, "in the time / Of fabled deities and false. A bard / Was I." The Pilgrim has found his "master and guide." Virgil leads him to the gates of hell, where the Pilgrim hesitates. After all, he isn't a great hero like Aeneas—how can he presume to enter this place? "Myself I deem not worthy," he says, "and none else / Will deem me."

But he *is* deemed worthy, for one reason above all: because he's a poet, because he will set down what he sees for others to read. In many ways *The Divine Comedy* rejects the skepticism about the possibilities of human knowledge represented elsewhere

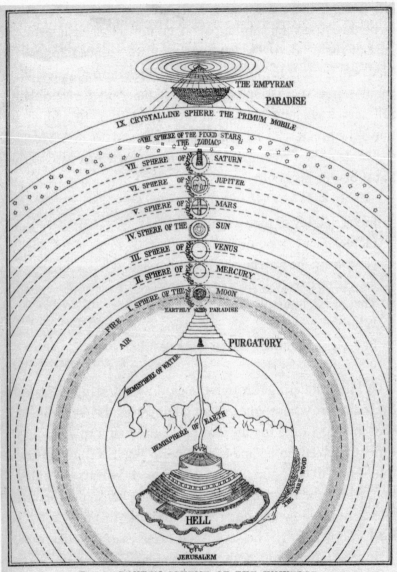

FIG. 4. DANTE'S SCHEME OF THE UNIVERSE
Slightly modified from Michelangelo Caetani, duca di Sermoneta, *La materia della Divina Commedia di Dante Allighieri dichiarata in VI tavole*, Monte Cassino, 1855.

in the Classics. (Dante knows Virgil only from his books, but knows him well enough to follow him into hell.) As one progresses through the circles of hell and up the mountain of purgatory and finally into heaven, the scale of Dante's ambition becomes clear. *The Divine Comedy* isn't just one of the great literary works of all time; it's one of the great human achievements of all time. All of medieval Florence is contained within it. And that's just the start. The entire universe, as Dante understood it, is there on the page.

That universe is a series of concentric circles. The outermost circles are Paradise, and at the center is earth. The Inferno stands within the center of that center. This universe is a closed system, and everything within the system stands in fixed relation to everything else. If Dante's achievement would be impossible now, it's not because we have no poets up to the task. It's because we no longer live in that universe. The universe we live in now is an infinity of points, and these points can be connected in an infinity of ways.

It's tempting, then, to see the *Comedy* as only the most elaborate —and the most beautiful—of speculative ventures into the unknowable. We understand now that the universe doesn't look like Dante's picture of it. But doubtless someone will eventually come along to demonstate the flaws in our own picture of the universe. In the meantime, these infinite points are our truth, just as those circles were Dante's truth. And he came closer than anyone else ever has to capturing his truth completely on the page.

I had read the *Inferno* several times and *Purgatory* once before that month, but I'd never read Dante's *Paradise*. I was surprised at what I found there. As the Pilgrim progresses toward the Empyrean,

Dante's language becomes less and less vivid. There is little of the startling imagery that makes the *Inferno* such a marvel. This seems to be by design, rather than a failure in the work. In the very last canto, the Pilgrim is given the chance to stand in direct contact with the light of the Divine. (By this point, the unbaptized Virgil has been left far behind, as has Dante's subsequent guide, Beatrice. This moment is completely unmediated.) Dante tries to explain to his readers what he has seen. But for once his poetic skill fails him.

> Thenceforward, what I saw,
> Was not for words to speak, nor memory's self
> To stand against such outrage on her skill.
> As one, who from a dream awaken'd, straight,
> All he hath seen forgets; yet still retains
> Impression of the feeling in his dream;
> E'en such am I.

Dante is among the most confident of all artists. He begins the poem by placing himself explicitly in the pantheon of great poets. So it is striking to see him end his great work on this humble note. Here we brush up again against the limits of the knowable. Perhaps it really is possible to gain an occasional glimpse beyond these limits. But even then the revelation is ineffable. Not only can it not be expressed to others; it can't be preserved except in the vaguest dreamlike ways.

The limits of human knowledge became a more practical concern to me once it was obvious that the doctors still had no idea what was causing my swelling. (They did seem to agree that it wasn't the plague.) Five years into remission, I no longer rushed to make an appointment every time something seemed slightly out of whack. But the issue was suddenly more pressing: I had a date.

At the beginning of the month, I'd gone to my fifth college reunion. I managed to keep the swelling down enough to leave me more or less presentable for the weekend. All I really had to worry about, then, was countless iterations of the same conversation:

Me: *What are you doing these days?*

Former Classmate: *I've just finished business school. And medical school. And I run a nonprofit that knits environmentally friendly sweaters for homeless babies. What are you doing, Chris?*

Me: *Well, I quit my job. I'm living in my parents' apartment. Mostly I sit around reading a lot of old books.*

Former Classmate: *I'm going to get a beer now.*

When the time came, things didn't go quite this badly. Over the course of the weekend, I found a dozen ways to answer this question that sounded, if not impressive, at least respectable. I mentioned the writing courses I was teaching at night, or the book reviews I published here and there. Mostly I told people about the novel I'd written, without mentioning that my agent had given up on sending it to publishers. Or else I said something about the memoir I was writing, of which I hadn't then written a word.

"What's it about?" a few people asked.

"It's about these books I'm reading."

"You're reading them now?"

"I mean, not right now. But, yeah."

"So you're writing a memoir about *now?*"

"I suppose you could think about it that way."

"So this conversation we're having could wind up in your book?"

"Well, probably not."

"Oh."

I don't remember exactly what answer I gave to L, a girl I'd had a crush on since we were undergrads, but she was kind enough to let it pass more or less unexamined. She was working in New York as a comedy writer, and I suggested that we should get together sometime. She agreed.

It was troubling, then, to wake up the day before our date and find my right eye swollen shut. I called the doctor's office and spoke with a physician's assistant, who told me to take an over-the-counter antihistamine and make an appointment to come in sometime soon. I followed her advice and hoped that the swelling would be down enough by the next day to allow me to keep my date. And indeed, the swelling was down a bit when I woke up. But now my lip was about an inch wide. I looked as if I'd been in a fistfight. I called the doctor again, expecting to have roughly the same conversation. But this time it went a bit differently.

"How's your eye?" the physician's assistant asked.

"It's better," I said. "But now my lip is swollen. I think my tongue might be a bit swollen, too."

A brief, nervous pause, and then: "How soon can you make it here?"

I arrived at the doctor's office, only a few blocks away, to find everyone taking my situation quite seriously. As I quickly learned, angioedema—swelling of the face and mouth—is a warning sign of anaphylactic shock. In other words, they were concerned that my throat would close up. After a few tests were done, I was given a heavy dose of something.

"You don't have to go back to work today, do you?" Dr. W asked before administering the shot.

"I'm self-employed," I told her. I couldn't even tell my doctor the truth.

"Good, because this may make you a bit drowsy."

I was nearly knocked out before I finished the short walk home, where I struggled to write an e-mail canceling my date before I passed out. For the rest of that day and much of the next, I passed into and out of consciousness. I'm not being facetious when I say that I felt as if I had some kind of revelation. Like Dante's glimpse of the divine, this revelation was gone in the very moment it arrived, leaving nothing but an impression of a feeling.

It had something to do with the idea that all the knowledge in the world is small recompense for the things we can't possibly know. There seem to be two contradictory facts about human nature. The first is that there is a sharp limit to what we can understand. Every time we expand the store of the known, this expansion serves to make the limit clearer and to make it obvious just how much—everything, really—lies beyond that limit. The second fact about human nature is that we want more than anything else to see beyond that limit. We aren't ones to stand at the cusp of death and say, as Socrates does, "Which is better, God only knows."

As it happens, my date would never be rescheduled, in part because I would spend so much of the next few months in the same state I was in then. Or worse: drugged, at once numb and in agonizing pain, unable to hold onto any one thought for more than a few moments. But I didn't know that yet, so I was almost able to enjoy that confused afternoon.

THE HARVARD CLASSICS

VERITAS

R H DANA JR

July, or "The Enjoyments of Life"

The allergist was unimpressed. Frankly, this didn't seem fair, since I'd been forced to wait until my outbreak had passed before making an appointment. I told him about my eye and my lip, but they didn't sound nearly as fearsome as they'd looked a few weeks before. I explained the history of the problem, which turned trifling once I put it into words. He asked a few questions and then consulted his notes, and I waited for him to tell me what was wrong.

It wasn't bugs, Dr. X said, but almost certainly some kind of allergic reaction. He would do some tests, but we were unlikely to isolate the cause. He prescribed something to take at night to prevent the swelling and something to take in the morning when the swelling arrived nonetheless. Everything about his attitude suggested that this was just life: the human body isn't a perfect machine; things go wrong.

There was something else, I said. My knee had been acting up. There seemed to be some fluid in it, and it hurt when I put weight on it. He rolled up my pants leg and confirmed that the knee was swollen.

"Have you been exercising?" he asked.

I'd been running a few days a week on a treadmill in the basement of my parents' building, and I'd been playing tennis during the weekends in Sag Harbor.

"You probably tweaked it," said Dr. X. Later, when people saw me on crutches, this is the word I would use. I had "tweaked" my knee. "I don't think it's related to your other issues. If it doesn't get better in another week or two, you might want to see an orthopedist."

But that wasn't all, I continued. Come to think of it—I hadn't thought of it until then—most of my joints hurt.

"OK," he said. "Why don't we start with these blood tests and go from there?"

He didn't quite tell me I was overdoing it, but his shrug suggested this. I left the office feeling frustrated. If the swelling was just something I had to live with, then I would. But I didn't want to live with it—not so much because of the discomfort itself as because of what it suggested.

My mother's father, whom I never met, contracted tuberculosis in his thirties and lived with emphysema as an older man. By the time of his death, he had the use of about one-quarter of one lung. He was very thin, in part because he hardly ate.

For all of his adult life, I've been told, he was frail; for much of
it he was sickly as well. All the pictures I have of him tend to
confirm this account. If photographs of my grandmother fix
her in my mind on a runway on the Rive Droite in the 1940s,
then photographs of her husband fix him in a kind of time-
less sanitarium. If this seems unfair, I should add that, for
several years after I entered my twenties, I assumed I would
join him there. I had come to the understanding that I would
spend most of my life weak and sick, cold and underfed. This
wasn't any great catastrophe: it was simply the condition of
my being in the world. But my cancer diagnosis, whatever else
it did, suggested another possibility. There was something
specifically wrong with me, and there was a plan to fix it. I'd
get better, or I'd die. This was comforting in its way: a stark
dichotomy instead of the middle ground of ongoing frailty. But
now the shrugs of Dr. X suggested that I was back to being
a sickly boy with a nameless complaint. I'd just have to live
with it.

I didn't want to accept all over again that I would go through
my life uncomfortably, that physical discomfort was simply my
lot. Of course I understood that there were far worse things than
being uncomfortable, worse things than a summer rash that kept
me up at night for a few months out of the year. I had witnessed
some of them. But it seemed to me that most people my age didn't
have these nagging worries. It seemed that too much of my life
had already been filled with illness, and I wanted to give it up.

"Considering how common illness is," Virginia Woolf once
wrote, "how tremendous the spiritual change that it brings, how
astonishing, when the lights of health go down, the undiscov-
ered countries that are then disclosed, . . . it becomes strange
indeed that illness has not taken its place with love, battle, and

jealousy among the prime themes of literature." The past century, with its Freudian and existential intimations that our very
being in the world is itself a kind of illness, remedied this lack
to some degree. But Woolf's point remains true with respect to
the vast majority of literary history. If the literature of illness
was a long time in coming, the Classics suggest that there has
long been a great literature of recovery.

Richard Henry Dana was twenty years old when measles struck
him. He was in his third year at Harvard. When he tried to return to his studies, he found his eyesight too weak to allow him
to read. So he set out to sea, determined "to cure, if possible, by
an entire change of life, and by a long absence from books and
study, a weakness of the eyes, which had obliged me to give up
my pursuits, and which no medical aid seemed likely to cure."
He doesn't mention his measles—I knew about them only
through the editor's introduction. He writes as though studying itself had been the cause of his weakened eyesight. At any
rate, we are done with this within the first paragraph; his story
is not about his illness, but about his recovery.

Dana might have signed on as a paying passenger, but instead
he took a job as a sailor on a ship called the *Pilgrim*. His memoir, *Two Years before the Mast* (1840), recounts this experience.
(The expression "before the mast" refers to crewmen who, unlike officers and passengers, are restricted to the front of the
ship.) His transition from Harvard man to sailing man really did
require an "entire change of life," beginning with his clothes:

> The change from the tight dress coat, silk cap and kid gloves
> of an undergraduate at Cambridge, to the loose duck trowsers,

JULY   133

checked shirt and tarpaulin hat of a sailor, though somewhat of a transformation, was soon made, and I supposed that I should pass very well for a jack tar. But it is impossible to deceive the practised eye in these matters; and while I supposed myself to be looking as salt as Neptune himself, I was, no doubt, known for a landsman by every one on board as soon as I hove in sight. A sailor has a peculiar cut to his clothes, and a way of wearing them which a green hand can never get. . . . Besides the points in my dress which were out of the way, doubtless my complexion and hands were enough to distinguish me from the regular salt, who, with a sunburnt cheek, wide step, and rolling gait, swings his bronzed and toughened hands athwartships, half open, as though just ready to grasp a rope.

Dana's language itself represents a kind of initiation. He's at once self-effacing and self-assured. We know from his tone that he is no longer a *green hand*, that he may in fact be *as salt as Neptune himself*, but we also know that he remembers what the feeling was like, that he will be a sympathetic guide for us landsmen.

Dana's first day at sea was a Sunday, but no notice of the Sabbath was given on board. There was too much work to be done. After the clothes, this was his first hint that the world of the ship was a different world, with different customs. *Two Years before the Mast* succeeds wonderfully in rendering this self-contained world, beginning with the hierarchy of captain ("lord paramount . . . he has no companion but his own dignity"), chief mate ("the prime minister, the official organ, and the active and superintending officer"), and second mate ("a dog's berth . . . neither officer nor man"), after which come the steward, the cook, and finally the crew. He gives a vivid description of the crew's life, with all its tedium.

"However much I was affected by the beauty of the sea, the bright stars, and the clouds driven swiftly over them," he writes about his first night on watch, "I could not but remember that I was separating myself from all the social and intellectual enjoyments of life."

This enjoyment was mostly replaced by labor. In good weather, on the open sea, that often meant busywork. "The discipline of the ship," Dana explains, "requires every man to be at work upon *something* when he is on deck . . . even if there is nothing to be done but to scrape the rust from the chain cables. In no state prison are the convicts more regularly set to work, and more closely watched." These long stretches of tedium are punctuated by short bursts of excitement and danger.

The *Pilgrim* was a trading ship; it sailed from Boston down to Cape Horn, and back up to the "western coast of North America." At the time that Dana sailed, the United States stretched as far as Missouri. Most of the land to the west was unsettled, and much of it belonged to Spain. The route the *Pilgrim* took was the quickest way to travel from east coast to west, but it was dangerous. Rounding Cape Horn was particularly treacherous, as Dana would learn firsthand. The ship set sail on August 15, 1834. It moved quickly through the tropics, where the weather was fine. By October it had crossed the equator and by November 4 it had reached the Cape. The next day, everything changed with the arrival of a "large black cloud."

Within moments, the *Pilgrim* was plunged into a heavy storm. Soon "all the forward part of her was under water; the sea pouring in through the bow-ports and hawse-hole and over the knightheads, threatening to wash everything overboard." The men on deck found themselves in water up to their waists. In the meantime, sleet and hail poured down heavily on them. "Here was an end to our fine prospects," Dana drily remarks.

By the next morning, the deck was completely covered with snow. The storms continued for several weeks, and during one of them a man fell overboard. Dana is especially moving when he writes about this moment. "Death is at all times solemn," he allows, "but never so much so as at sea."

> A man dies on shore; his body remains with his friends, and "the mourners go about the streets;" but when a man falls overboard at sea and is lost, there is a suddenness in the event, and a difficulty in realizing it, which give to it an air of awful mystery. A man dies on shore—you follow his body to the grave, and a stone marks the spot. You are often prepared for the event. There is always something which helps you to realize it when it happens, and to recall it when it has passed. A man is shot down by your side in battle, and the mangled body remains an object, and a real evidence; but at sea, the man is near you—at your side—you hear his voice, and in an instant he is gone, and nothing but a vacancy shows his loss.

When it finally arrived in California, the *Pilgrim* began the work for which it had set sail, which was trading for goods, mostly hides, to be brought back to the east coast. Dana spent the next year and half in a series of Spanish and Indian settlements—Monterrey, Santa Barbara, San Diego, San Francisco. At each stop, he lived with several other crewmen in a hide-house— "a large building, made of rough boards"—where they cured hides for the return trip. "Here was a change in my life as complete as it had been sudden," he writes.

As described in the book, this was a period of great uncertainty for Dana. The crew was entirely at the captain's mercy, for he wouldn't start their return leg until he was satisfied with their haul. Dana was on land for weeks at a time, and he worried that he would never get back to Boston, or that he would get back too late to return to school, too late to have any career but as a sailor. Eventually, he worked his way onto another ship, the *Alert*, which left California in May 1836, having acquired "forty thousand hides, thirty thousand horns, besides several barrels of otter and beaver skins."

The *Alert* arrived back at Cape Horn in July, which was the worst month of the year for sailing there. The captain waited another month before even attempting the passage, and then the helmsman came close to striking an iceberg and destroying the ship. Once the *Alert* did get around the Cape, the trip north in the Atlantic was uneventful, and Dana reached Boston in September 1838, a little more than two years after setting out. He returned to Harvard, where his experiences made him a hero among his new classmates.

Two Years before the Mast has a wonderful postscript, called "Twenty Four Years After," describing a trip Dana took to California late in 1859. In the intervening years, steamships had replaced sailing ships as the primary means of ocean travel. On this second trip, Dana traveled on the steamship *Golden Gate*, which was "gay with crowds of passengers, and lighting the sea for miles around with the glare of her signal lights of red, green, and white, and brilliant with lighted saloons and staterooms." And it went not by way of

Cape Horn but over Panama (the canal had not yet been built, but metal steamships could be transported across the isthmus). From there, the passage took only a few days. Before long, the ship arrived in San Francisco Bay. Twenty-four years earlier, the place had been a nearly abandoned Indian trading outpost. "Not only the neighborhood of our anchorage," Dana writes, "but the entire region of the great bay, was a solitude."

What he finds now is unrecognizable. At the former nearly uninhabited anchoring-ground of the hide ships, he sees "a city of one hundred thousand inhabitants. Clocks tolled the hour of midnight from its steeples, but the city was alive from the salute of our guns, spreading the news that the fortnightly steamer had come, bringing mails and passengers from the Atlantic world."

A few days later, the ship arrived in San Diego, where Dana searched the shoreline for one of the hide-houses in which he had lived and traded during his first stay in California. But there was nothing. He writes:

I wished to be alone, so I let the other passengers go up to the town, and was quietly pulled ashore in a boat, and left to myself. The recollections and the emotions all were sad, and only sad. . . . The past was real. The present, all about me, was unreal, unnatural, repellent. I saw the big ships lying in the stream, the Alert, the California, the Rosa, with her Italians; then the handsome Ayacucho, my favorite; the poor, dear old Pilgrim, the home of hardship and hopelessness; the boats passing to and fro; the cries of the sailors at the capstan or falls; the peopled beach; the large hide-houses with their gangs of men; and the Kanakas interspersed everywhere. All, all were gone! not a vestige to mark where one hide-house stood.

Within the Harvard Classics, Dana's memoir comes immediately after the *Odyssey* (c. 700 BCE). Beside that poem— beside most of the Classics, frankly—*Two Years before the Mast* stands as a minor work. But this one passage has remained with me as much as anything I read all year. It may be that more had changed in the life of the sailor in the twenty-four years between Dana's two trips than in the twenty-five hundred years between Odysseus's last voyage and Dana's first. There was steam now. Never again would a commercial ship need to wait for weeks, like the *Pilgrim* and the *Alert,* for the wind to allow a trip to continue. There were "staterooms" onboard the *Golden Gate,* as if the great Homeric banquet hall of Ithaca had been moved onto the ship itself.

This isn't all that strikes me about the passage. The first edition of *Two Years before the Mast* was published in 1840, not long after Dana's return to Boston. The book made him an intellectual celebrity. He had graduated from Harvard by then and had begun practicing law. He worked in particular on the rights of sailors, a cause to which he dedicated much of his life. (His intention in starting the book, in fact, was to shed light on the conditions of the common sailor.) He would go on to act as counsel to a number of fugitive slaves and to enter politics; and Lincoln named him the U.S. district attorney for Massachusetts. It's impossible to know what success Dana would have had if he'd never had measles, never been forced to leave Harvard. But we can see that the great man he did become was shaped by those two years before the mast, years during which he traded all of the "enjoyments of life" for drudgery and manual labor.

By the time Dana made his second trip to California, he was famous there for his portrayal of the place in its earlier days. He was stopped in every town and asked about that time. He was treated as a great dignitary. And yet there he is offshore at San Diego, searching for a glimpse of the shacks where he had worked tanning hides and longing for home. The very ease of the steamship seems to sadden him. Dana must have recognized how much he owed to illness and hardship. Now that he has earned a comfortable passage, he wants the hardship back. It's the only thing that's real to him.

John Stuart Mill's *Autobiography* (1873), the other memoir I read that month as I fell back into my own illness, also centers on recovery. Mill had one of the most unusual educations ever recorded, guided by his father, the Benthamite philosopher and historian James Mill. "I have no remembrance of the time when I began to learn Greek," the younger Mill writes in his *Autobiography*. "I have been told that it was when I was three years old." Within a few years, he had read all of Herodotus and the first six of Plato's dialogues in the original Greek. ("The last dialogue . . . would have been better omitted," he adds, seemingly serious, "as it was totally impossible I should understand it.") At eight, Mill took up Latin. He also began to learn arithmetic, which was his least favorite subject.

However, the greatest influence on him was not anything he found in books but rather the time he spent with his father. The two sat side by side each day at the same writing desk. Mill read Xenophon and Diogenes Laertius while his father wrote a *History of India*. They had no Greek-English lexicon, so the son would interrupt his father's work each time he came to an unfamiliar word. The two took walks together each day, and during these walks John Stuart summarized for his father his previous day's reading. Mill explains, "In these frequent talks about the books I read, he used, as opportunity offered, to give me explanations and ideas respecting civilization, government, morality, mental cultivation, which he required me afterwards to restate to him in my own words."

Mill gives a rather intimidating portrait of the man, although he clearly admired his father greatly.

In his views of life he partook of the character of the Stoic, the Epicurean, and the Cynic, not in the modern but the ancient sense of the word. In his personal qualities the Stoic predominated. His standard of morals was Epicurean, inasmuch as it was utilitarian, taking as the exclusive test of right and wrong, the tendency of actions to produce pleasure or pain. But he had (and this was the Cynic element) scarcely any belief in pleasure; at least in his later years, of which alone, on this point, I can speak confidently. He was not insensible to pleasures; but he deemed very few of them worth the price which, at least in the present state of society, must be paid for them. The greater number of miscarriages in life, he considered to be attributable to the overvaluing of pleasures. Accordingly, temperance, in the large sense intended by the Greek philosophers—stopping short at the point of moderation in all indulgences—was with him, as with them, almost the central point of educational precept.

Throughout this time, many of the greatest British thinkers—including Bentham, Hume, and Ricardo—frequented the Mills' house, and John Stuart seems to have participated in their discussions from a very early age. At fifteen, he started reading Bentham's work, and he determined to become a reformer in

Bentham's utilitarian mold. "My conception of my own happiness was entirely identified with this object," he writes.

When Mill reached the age of twenty, he took a position at the East India Company, where his father worked. Like his father, Mill treated this as a day job around which to do his real work. He contributed to the same reviews for which his father and his father's friends wrote. He was very much a utilitarian, rejecting traditional religious morality and believing instead that the greatest moral good was to maximize happiness or pleasure and to minimize pain. (During his era he was, by his own account, "one of the very few examples, in this country, of one who has, not thrown off religious belief, but never had it.") It was along these lines that he was driven to reform society. He and his circle wanted to be the British counterparts of the French *philosophes*.

"I conceive that the description so often given of a Benthamite," Mill writes, "as a mere reasoning machine, though extremely inapplicable to most of those who have been designated by that title, was during two or three years of my life not altogether untrue of me." But then he came to what he calls "a crisis in my mental history."

In the fall of 1826, Mill woke from his machinelike existence "as from a dream." He went through a period of what he calls "a dull state of nerves, such as everybody is occasionally liable to; unsusceptible to enjoyment or pleasurable excitement." This crisis might not have been overly serious for Mill, except that while he was in this state, he asked himself a question that changed everything:

"Suppose that all your objects in life were realized; that all the changes in institutions and opinions which you are looking forward to, could be completely effected at this very instant: would this be a great joy and happiness to you?" And an irrepressible self-consciousness distinctly answered, "No!" At this my heart sank within me: the whole foundation on which my life was constructed fell down. All my happiness was to have been found in the continual pursuit of this end. The end had ceased to charm, and how could there ever again be any interest in the means? I seemed to have nothing left to live for.

Given his background, it comes as little surprise that he attempted first to read his way out of this crisis. But, like Dana, Mill learned that his old studies wouldn't help him. He turned to his favorite books, to "those memorials of past nobleness and greatness," only to find that "I read them now without feeling, or with the accustomed feeling minus all its charm; and I became persuaded, that my love of mankind, and of excellence for its own sake, had worn itself out."

Until then, Mill had brought nearly every question in his life to his father. But James Mill, he now decided, was the last person to whom he could bring this particular problem. "Everything convinced me that he had no knowledge of any such mental state as I was suffering from, and that even if he could be made to understand it, he was not the physician who could heal it." Moreover, given his father's singular role in his education, how could he now explain that this education had failed him in some important way, especially "when the failure was probably irremediable, and, at all events, beyond the power of his remedies"?

Throughout the winter of 1826–1827, Mill continued his work, "mechanically, by the mere force of habit." Many times he asked himself how long he could go on living in such a state. He concluded that he couldn't endure it more than a year.

Of all the autobiographies included in the Harvard Classics, none contains anything quite like this moment. In the years before his conversion, Augustine *enjoyed* his life of sin; this was precisely what made it so difficult to give up. To find that life no longer gives you pleasure—not that you are in misery, like Manfred or Our Lady's Child, but simply that you no longer feel pleasure—is a rather modern predicament, because it's a modern idea that life ought to be designed for pleasure.

Mill had been trained in analytic thinking, but he did not have a proper object to which to apply his skill. He was, he said, like a well-made ship with a rudder but no sail. The result was excessive self-consciousness. "Ask yourself whether you are happy," he concluded, "and you cease to be so."

In the end, no single event saved Mill from his "mental crisis." In fact, his melancholy would return sporadically throughout his life. But during this first bout he was helped by reading the memoirs of the French writer Marmontel. He came to an account of the death of Marmontel's father and found himself moved to tears. After that emotional outbreak, Mill writes, "my being grew lighter. The oppression of the thought that all feeling was dead within me, was gone." He no longer felt like a "stock or a stone."

His progress from there was gradual. First he found himself capable of taking basic pleasure in "the ordinary incidents of life." Sunshine, books, conversation—they once again gave him enjoyment, "not intense, but sufficient for cheerfulness." From there, he came to realize "that there was, once more, excitement, though of a moderate kind, in exerting myself for my opinions, and for the public good."

The key to Mill's initial emotional response was that it had been spontaneous. He had not picked up Marmontel's book in order to be moved out of his depression. He had picked it up for unrelated reasons and only then found himself being moved. This experience changed his outlook on life in several ways. He still felt, along with the utilitarians, that happiness was the chief end in life. But now he believed "that this end was only to be attained by not making it the direct end." The only people who are truly happy are those who set their own happiness aside, "who have their minds fixed on some object other than their own happiness; on the happiness of others, on the improvement of mankind, even on some art or pursuit, followed not as a means, but as itself an ideal end." Those who aim at something else besides their own happiness will find happiness "by the way." He concludes that "the enjoyments of life . . . are sufficient to make it a pleasant thing, when they are taken *en passant*, without being made a principal object. Once make them so, and they are immediately felt to be insufficient."

Mill uses the same expression—"the enjoyments of life"—that Dana had used twenty years earlier when describing the feeling of sailing away from Boston. There is a paradox here, of course. One must accept happiness as a goal but also give up seeking it in order to achieve it. And there is a deeper paradox as well: Mill's period of profound unhappiness was necessary for him to discover the proper path to happiness, just as Dana's two years before the mast made him the man he became. Mill acknowledges this conflict. He now sees the hardships of life as a necessary component of happiness. He even comes to wonder "whether, if the reformers of society and government could succeed in their objects, and every person in the community were free and in a state of physical comfort, the pleasures of life, being no longer kept up by struggle and privation, would cease to be pleasures."

Now, it's easy enough to say that life's difficulties make the better moments more meaningful; the idea can even be used as an excuse to stand by and allow people to suffer. While I was sick, I often heard people suggest that my illness would make me "stronger." Bullshit, I thought. And so I still think. But I also think this: if you design your life around pleasure, life will teach you eventually to do otherwise. Your comfort, especially your physical comfort, isn't under your control, so you'd better find something else to work at.

Mill took another lesson from his experience. For the first time, he "gave its proper place, among the prime necessities of human well-being, to the internal culture of the individual." All of his education had been in the reading of history, philosophy, and rhetoric, with the aim of equipping him to have an effect on the world around him, to be a "reformer." But now he saw that how one acts in the world isn't everything; there is also how one feels inside. I imagine that this evolution in Mill's thinking is a large part of the reason for his place in the Five-Foot Shelf. His discovery about "internal culture" is the same idea advocated by Emerson, the idea so important to Eliot's motives in putting the Harvard Classics together.

Through this evolution, Mill came, in theory at least, to appreciate the importance of poetry and art, even if he had not yet felt their power through personal experience. The only "imaginative art" in which he had taken pleasure up to this time was music, and even that pleasure was "suspended during the gloomy period." But in the period immediately after his "crisis," Mill read Wordsworth for the first time. He had, during his depression, read Byron with the active hope that it would help his

recovery. But now he read Wordsworth without any particular aim. He found that Wordsworth's descriptions of nature
spoke to his own appreciation for nature, but he also found
something more important to him than this rendering of the
physical world:

> What made Wordsworth's poems a medicine for my state of
> mind, was that they expressed, not mere outward beauty, but
> states of feeling, and of thought coloured by feeling, under the
> excitement of beauty. They seemed to be the very culture of the
> feelings, which I was in quest of. In them I seemed to draw from
> a Source of inward joy, of sympathetic and imaginative pleasure,
> which could be shared in by all human beings; which had no
> connexion with struggle of imperfection, but would be made
> richer by every improvement in the physical or social condition
> of mankind. From them I seemed to learn what would be the
> perennial sources of happiness, when all the greater evils of life
> shall have been removed.

Mill also found that Wordsworth's experience had been much
like his own. They both had "felt that the first freshness of youthful enjoyment of life was not lasting." This gave him the idea
that his great crisis was actually rather unspectacular, that everyone was uncomfortable in his own way. But Wordsworth, he
thought, had found "compensation" for this loss in a deeper
feeling for life. Now, Wordsworth pointed the way for Mill to
do the same.

After reading the rest of Mill's *Autobiography*, which describes
his adult life as one of the great liberal thinkers of the nineteenth
century, I came back again to Mill's experience with Wordsworth.
Later in the year, I would have an eerily similar experience with

the same poet, but for now, I was interested in the word "compensation." It doesn't suggest that the losses and hardships of life can be undone. Nor does it suggest that these losses and hardships are somehow "worth it" in the end. But it does suggest that if we know where to look we will be given something in return for them, and that we may even come to prize that compensation, the thing that our suffering bought us, more than life's enjoyments.

THE HARVARD CLASSICS

VERI
TAS

ARNOLD

August, or "Go to Grass"

My father's family owns an old farmhouse in upstate New York. The Behas came to the area from Germany in the middle of the nineteenth century, and they settled in this thoroughly rural area to work as farmers and later as schoolteachers. When the widowed matriarch of the family—my grandfather's grandmother—moved downstate, she attempted to sell the home that her husband and his father had built by hand. This effort having failed, the house remained in the family, as it has ever since. We make one or two trips each summer to the place that we call simply "the Farm," though no farming has been done on its land in a century.

On the day that I planned to make the five-hour drive there with my brother Jim and his fiancée, Alyson, I went first to the orthopedist. He was the third doctor I'd seen in a month. In the weeks since my trip to the allergist, my knee had not improved. In fact, it had gotten noticeably worse, although I'd stopped working out on it. I explained to Dr. Y everything that I'd already explained to Drs. W and X. He rolled up my pants and pushed my leg in a few different places, asking for my response each time.

"Does this hurt?" Dr. Y asked.

"No."

"Does this hurt?"

"No."

"Does this hurt?"

"Maybe?"

"Does this . . ."

Dr. Y gave a knowing smile when he heard me scream.

"You've torn your meniscus," he said.

Then he took out a plastic model of a knee and showed me what the meniscus was. He explained the different types of tears that were possible and the ways they might be fixed. I would have to come in for an MRI to determine if I needed surgery. I told him I'd be leaving town for a few days, and he said the test could wait, so long as I kept off my feet.

As if this very warning had weakened me, I found myself unable to walk home from the appointment, though I'd gone there on foot just an hour earlier. I took a cab home and waited for Jim to pick me up. During the drive that afternoon, I sat in the back of the car with my leg propped up and a bag of ice on my knee. Once we arrived, I limped inside. Near the foot of the stairs sat an old wooden cane that had belonged to my grandfather. I used it to get around for the next few days.

We weren't there for much more than a weekend, but I had packed two volumes of the Harvard Classics: *English Essays— Sidney to Macaulay* and *Essays—English and American*. I hoped to get as much reading done as possible during our stay. With all that had happened so far during the year, I had fallen a bit off pace. I needed to finish more than a volume a week from then on if I was going to complete the Shelf by New Year's. If nothing else, convalescing from an injury might give me a chance to catch up.

When my brother and sister and I were younger, these trips to the Farm were always preceded by outings to a small bookstore around the corner from our house in the city. Once we arrived upstate, we spent most of each day hiking around the property or exploring the two barns behind the house. The smaller of the two held my grandfather's first car, a Pontiac from the 1930s. The interior was rusted out, and there was a tear in the front seat that exposed a menacing spring, but this car seemed miraculous to my siblings and me, and we could spend entire afternoons playing inside it. The other barn held frightening and thrilling pieces of old farm equipment. Most of it was being stored for neighbors, though a few odd tools dated back to my family's farming days.

After dark we came inside and sat together quietly in the living room, reading whatever books we had picked out before our departure. I liked to think that our ancestors had spent their summer nights the same way. There was a television in the corner, which required constant manipulation of its antennae for even the fuzziest reception, but it was left off except for the half hour each night when my grandmother watched the evening news. On these trips to the Farm I truly fell in love with reading and first got the idea that I wanted to write. At certain moments throughout the day, everything got very quiet, and this quiet called out to be filled by acts of the imagination. At night, as I lay in bed, I plotted out the books that I would one day write.

Only now do I recognize something else those trips must have given me: my sense of the past as staying with us, sometimes hidden but always there. First, there was the house itself, which is filled with relics from an earlier time. There are old photographs and daguerreotypes, letters and journals, and even a pair of ancient eyeglasses. In the kitchen is a wood-burning stove, and in the parlor are an upright piano and a small organ with a stack of sheet music. The parlor itself is like a period room from a historical museum. Hardly any furniture has been replaced since the family moved out. But the room doesn't feel preserved; it feels lived in.

Then there are the neighbors. I've spent most of my life in Manhattan, a place famous for its headlong rush into the future. But on both sides of our family's house are other farms that have been in their families for generations. As a child, I could walk to one of these farms and watch its owners milk their cows, just as their parents and grandparents had done. Of course, the method had changed, but the essential task, the rhythmic necessity of milking the herd twice each day, remained the same.

Just a mile down Fish Creek Road stands the Church of Saints Peter and Paul. Behind it is a small graveyard and in that graveyard is Matthias Beha, the first in my line to be buried in American soil. He's there with his wife, Mary Anna, and about half a dozen other family members, some of whom were just a few weeks old when they were put into the ground. On the Sunday of each weekend we spent at the Farm, we would go to Mass there, and afterward we would walk around back to see Matthias and the others. They no longer hold Masses at this church: there are neither enough priests nor enough parishioners to sustain it. My parents now drive to a church in the next town. But no matter what else we do during our stays at the Farm, we always go back to visit the family.

The Harvard Classics aren't arranged chronologically. In fact, they have no particular order at all. There are benefits to this

format. Reading works from vastly different eras, sometimes the later ones first, emphasizes all that remains unchanged about the human experience, about the questions we ask ourselves and the stories we tell. It is as if all of history were there at the same time, a kind of physical space to be explored at will. But there are also costs to this lack of order. Read from beginning to end, the Shelf fails to give much sense of a tradition progressing over time, modifying itself to meet the particular challenges of each new era.

There are exceptions to this lack of chronology, most notably the anthologies, which take a particular literary genre and follow it through most of its history. The two volumes I'd brought with me to the Farm that weekend trace the essay in English from the Elizabethan age to the end of the nineteenth century.

Michel de Montaigne, the French writer of the 1500s who virtually invented the modern essay, withdrew from society before he began his major work. As a landowning aristocrat, he could afford to do so. But most of the great English essayists were very much men of the world, whether by disposition or necessity. Sir Philip Sidney and Joseph Addison both served as members of Parliament and diplomats from the royal court. Jonathan Swift was involved in Tory politics and appointed dean of Saint Patrick's, Dublin. These two volumes include an essay by John Henry Newman, the nineteenth-century Catholic cardinal, and another by William Ellery Channing, the leader of the Unitarian movement. They also include essays by writers famous for work in other forms—Ben Jonson, Coleridge, Shelley, William Makepeace Thackeray, Edgar Allan Poe.

The essays themselves often consider important topics of the day—the education of women, the "elevation" of the "laboring classes." Some are passing attempts—"essays" in the original sense of the word—written in a casual style about a seemingly fleeting interest. Many take as their subject the life and work of fellow writers: Addison writes about a visit to Westminster Abbey; Samuel Johnson writes about Addison; Swift writes about the "art of conversation"; Thackeray writes about Swift. The result is that these two volumes of essays offer not just a history of the form, but a history of the culture and society that produced it. Reading these essays, I had the same feeling I have when reading letters and journals found in drawers at the farm, where major historical moments are mentioned in passing as the stuff of everyday life. "President McKinley shot yesterday," one such entry notes, amid a list of recent household purchases.

These volumes are also among the few instances in the Classics where one can see literary history in all its dynamism, as a force that pushes itself forward through a combination of outward observation and self-criticism. "Whoever wishes to attain an English style, familiar but not coarse, and elegant but not ostentatious," Johnson writes, "must give his days and nights to the volumes of Addison." And this is very much the sense that one gets in progressing through these volumes—of writers reading each other, their writing a kind of ongoing conversation with one another and with the culture at large.

The most common subject here, in fact, is the literary tradition itself, beginning with the very first essay included, Sir Philip Sidney's "The Defense of Poesy" (1579), in which he argues that the form has been the means by which great the ideas of philosophy, history, and ethics first make their way into our culture. The philosopher "teacheth obscurely," Sidney argues, "so as the learned only can understand him; that is to say, he teacheth them that are already taught." In contrast, the poet is a "popular philosopher," making ideas available to all. In Sidney's time, the term "poetry" meant not just verse but imaginative writing in general, so his full argument—that the history of ideas is made available to all through literature—is the very one advanced by the Harvard Classics. To make his point, in fact, he uses an example included in the Shelf: "Aesop's tales give good proof; whose pretty allegories, stealing under the formal tales of beasts, make many, more beastly than beasts, begin to hear the sound of virtue from those dumb speakers."

Sidney's essay was written in response to an attack by one of his contemporaries, and this fact adds to the sense of these essays as an ongoing conversation. Ben Jonson writes about Shakespeare and Bacon. Coleridge, like Sidney, takes up the more general topic of "poesy." Shelley makes his famous declaration that the poet is the "unacknowledged legislator of the age." And the conversation continues, until we reach the nineteenth-century poet and critic Matthew Arnold.

It might be fairly said that without Arnold, there would be no Harvard Classics. After Emerson, he was the chief precursor of the genteel tradition. He was also the great modern champion of the canon: the idea of our literary heritage as representing mankind at its best, something not just for academics or dilettantes, but for everyone. "More and more mankind will discover," Arnold says in "The Study of Poetry" (1888), which was written to introduce an anthology of English poems, "that we have to turn to poetry to interpret life for us, to console us, to sustain us. Without poetry, our science will appear incomplete; and most of what now passes with us for religion and philosophy will be replaced by poetry."

Arnold is one of the few writers whose defense of literature rises to the standards of literature itself. He warns against historical readings of poetry, arguing instead for just the kind of disorder created by the lack of chronology in the Five-Foot Shelf. "The course of development of a nation's language, thought, and poetry, is profoundly interesting," Arnold admits. But he believes we must be wary of mistaking historical significance for intrinsic worth. We shouldn't read a great work of literature in order to distinguish its place in the tradition: "If he is a real classic, if his work belongs to the class of the very best (for this is the true and right meaning of the word classic, classical), then the great thing for us is to feel and enjoy his work as deeply as ever we can, and to appreciate the wide difference between it and all work which has not the same high character."

As these last words suggest, Arnold believes in tradition not as a historical context but as a kind of measuring stick that reveals the intrinsic worth of a work. Every time he reads a line of poetry, it seems, Arnold is judging it against what he knows of Homer, Chaucer, or Shakespeare. If it doesn't meet this standard—as, of course, it usually doesn't—then it should be discarded: so long as the true Classics exist, there is little sense in spending much time on the untrue or even the half-true.

Arnold spent his working life as England's inspector of schools. He didn't always think much of the job, which required a great deal of traveling, but it allowed him to see more of the world around him than many men of letters ever do, and it made him think about the dissemination of culture to all stations of life and throughout his country, not just to a privileged class in the cultural capital. In this way, he was another of the English essayists whose writing was informed by engagement with the world.

There is just one writer in these volumes who conforms to Montaigne's model of retreat from the world: Henry David Thoreau. He seems to retire not just from society but from tradition; he is in conversation not with fellow writers but with himself. I've always been a great admirer of Thoreau's writing, and it was at the Farm that I was introduced to him many years before. I first read "Walden" after a day spent at our own pond, dug and filled seventy years ago by my great-grandfather. City boy though I was, I could still imagine in those quiet evenings that I shared some of Thoreau's spirit, that some part of me stood apart from the world into which I'd been born. This was the kind of writer I imagined myself being when I thought of such things on languorous summer evenings in my childhood— not the writer who engaged with society, but the writer who chose the pleasures of solitary contemplation.

"I wish to speak a word for Nature," Thoreau writes in "Walking" (1851), the essay included here, "for absolute freedom and wildness, as contrasted with a freedom and culture merely civil,—to regard man as an inhabitant, or a part and parcel of Nature, rather than a member of society."

It wasn't until my freshman year in college that I discovered this essay, but I've read it every few months since then, perhaps three dozen times in all. In the undergraduate class in nonfiction writing that I taught after finishing graduate school, I included the essay on my syllabus every semester. It seems to capture all that is best about Thoreau's writing and his relationship to the world around him. Like his mentor Emerson, Thoreau falls into the great category of learned men who are ultimately suspicious of learning, or at least acutely aware of its limits. He begins his essay with an almost academic consideration of the etymology of the verb "to saunter":

which word is beautifully derived from "idle people who roved about the country, in the Middle Ages, and asked charity, under pretence of going à la Sainte Terre," to the Holy Land, till the children exclaimed, "There goes a Sainte-Terrer," a Saunterer, a Holy-Lander. They who never go to the Holy Land in their walks, as they pretend, are indeed mere idlers and vagabonds; but they who do go there are saunterers in the good sense, such as I mean. Some, however, would derive the word from *sans terre,* without land or a home, which, therefore, in the good sense, will mean, having no particular home, but equally at home everywhere. For this is the secret of successful saunter-ing. He who sits still in a house all the time may be the greatest vagrant of all; but the saunterer, in the good sense, is no more vagrant than the meandering river, which is all the while sedu-lously seeking the shortest course to the sea. But I prefer the first, which, indeed, is the most probable derivation. For every walk is a sort of crusade, preached by some Peter the Hermit in us, to go forth and reconquer this Holy Land from the hands of the Infidels.

There is something wonderfully half-hearted about that "which, indeed, is the most probable variation." Thoreau couldn't care less which derivation is actually correct; the point he is mak-ing is emotional or poetic. He will keep to his etymologist's defi-nition of the word for as long as it's of use, but discard it when it seems to pull in the wrong direction.

In order to preserve his spirits, Thoreau goes on to explain, he must spend at least four hours a day out walking. He can't stay inside for a single afternoon without "acquiring some rust." Thoreau's essay is one of the last in the second volume I read that weekend. By the time I finished it, I had read about nine hundred pages in the span of two days. In that time, I'd hardly

left my armchair in a corner of the sitting room, and I was acquiring some rust myself. We were leaving the next day, and if
I was going to make a trip down to the graveyard, this afternoon
would be my last chance. I stood up, leaning on my grandfather's
cane, and started walking.

About halfway to the church, my mother, my brother, and I
were met by our neighbor's dog, who's missing one of his front
legs. He joined us for the rest of the trip, hopping along much
more quickly and ably than I could. It was cool, as it usually is
there even at the height of summer, with a brisk breeze and a
wide-open sky. The air was redolent with the smell of hay left
out to dry. After all that time inside, I was struck more power-
fully than I usually am by the beauty of the landscape. We came
over the hill, and the old church came into view. I was struggling
by then, but I gave no thought to turning back.

There is a passage in Thoreau's essay I have always found
beautiful, and I was especially struck by it that weekend: it ran
through my mind while we walked. It contains a bit of the epistemological humility of Socrates, but only Thoreau could have
written it. "We have heard of a Society for the Diffusion of Useful Knowledge," he writes. "Methinks there is equal need of a
Society for the Diffusion of Useful Ignorance, what we will call
Beautiful Knowledge, a knowledge useful in a higher sense: for
what is most of our boasted so-called knowledge but a conceit
that we know something, which robs us of the advantage of our
actual ignorance?"

What we call knowledge is often our positive ignorance; ignorance our negative knowledge. By long years of patient industry and reading of the newspapers,—for what are the libraries
of science but files of newspapers?—a man accumulates a

myriad facts, lays them up in his memory, and then when in some spring of his life he saunters abroad into the Great Fields of thought, he, as it were, goes to grass like a horse and leaves all his harness behind in the stable. I would say to the Society for the Diffusion of Useful Knowledge, sometimes,—Go to grass. You have eaten hay long enough.

On that day, with my leg throbbing, I couldn't make the usual round of the graveyard. But Matthias and Mary Anna were among the founders of the parish, and their graves are in the first row behind the church. Their stones have been amazingly well preserved, though we've never done anything to contribute to this preservation. The marble is still white and the names and dates are perfectly legible. I stood there in front of them for a few minutes, leaning on my grandfather's cane, before I turned around to head back. By the time I reached the house, I could hardly stand, but I didn't mind: I had gone to grass.

This all seemed a bit less romantic when I woke the next morning to discover that I couldn't find my knee. I don't mean that I couldn't see the outline of my kneecap beneath all the swelling— I'd reached that point several days earlier. I mean that when I probed by hand at the middle of my leg I could locate no firm bone beneath the squishy fluid. I could neither straighten nor bend my leg; the joint was fixed in an awkward in-between position.

In the city two days later, the technician had a similar problem when he prepared me for my MRI. He had to use my other leg as a guide to line my knee up for the machine. When the pictures came back a few days later, Dr. Y scheduled surgery.

I'd brought my grandfather's cane back from the farm, but it was no good by this point. I was instead using a pair of crutches that my brother had bought for me on our first day back in town. The only other time in my life that I'd been on crutches was during the weeks before my cancer diagnosis, when my ankles blew up inexplicably. Because I was so sick and weak at the time, I could hardly get myself around on them. I had to stop every few steps, and the tops of the crutches tore the skin away from the insides of my arms. Since then, I've associated crutches with more than just injuries. As in a Victorian novel, they suggest an overarching, almost moral infirmity.

Sure enough, things started happening to my body as soon as I started using crutches again. I was visited with an eerily familiar sense of physical malaise and exhaustion. Not just my knee but all my joints—my entire body, really—ached. I started having strange lapses in my short-term memory. Several times that week I found myself lying in bed when someone arrived in my room with something I didn't remember asking for. I was traveling back to that other country, illness.

Though it was increasingly clear that there was something wrong beyond a torn meniscus, I didn't want to admit as much to my family, who had had enough to worry about that year. I couldn't help thinking that my problems were largely psychological, that I had turned into someone for whom every minor injury must become a grave crisis. But if I didn't tell anyone about it, if I kept the crisis to myself, so my thinking went, it couldn't possibly be made up. Is there such a thing as closet hypochondria?

A few days before the surgery, I went to Dr. W for my pre-op exam. I'd spent a great deal of time in her office of late, so this appointment seemed like a formality.

"We have to send you to the lab for blood work," said Dr. W.

"I was just at the lab," I told her. "Dr. X sent me for blood work. Can't we use that?"

She left the room to take a look at the tests done a few weeks earlier by the allergist. In a few minutes she came back.

"You should be all right for your surgery," she said.

"Great," I said.

Almost offhandedly, she added, "What did Dr. X prescribe for your Lyme disease?"

"Excuse me?"

We spent some time discussing the options. Dr. Y was called, and he confirmed that we should go ahead with the surgery. Dr. W gave me a prescription for a painkiller and another for an antibiotic. Then I made my way home on my crutches.

The next day, I found that I could no longer read. When I looked at a page the letters refused to cohere into words; the words refused to form sentences. The printing was a code whose key I didn't possess. This problem seemed related to my short-term memory, which had gotten worse over the preceding days.

"Brain fog," said Dr. Z, the rheumatologist I visited a few days later. This sounded like something in a science-fiction movie. He assured me that these cognitive symptoms would pass; nonetheless, the term "brain fog" troubled me.

I knew a bit about Lyme disease before my diagnosis. It's a bacterial disease spread by deer ticks, and the area where my family stays in Sag Harbor is overrun with deer. From time to time during my childhood, my mother, Mimi, and my sister would each in turn find tick bites on their bodies, and these bites developed the bull's-eye rash that indicates Lyme disease. They suffered for a short time from flu-like symptoms, which were cleared up quickly by antibiotics. I also knew that the disease could become more serious if left long untreated (as it had apparently been in my case); a childhood classmate of my sister's had missed a full year of school with a bad case of it. But the risk of "brain fog" was new to me.

Except for my surgery and a few more trips to Dr. Z, I didn't leave the apartment for another month after that. I have never experienced anything remotely like the pain I was in during those weeks, which was considerably worse than the pain that had come with my cancer. I spent my days waiting until I could take the next dose of Percocet and my nights waiting for the sleeping pills to kick in.

Only a few months before, I had seen someone suffer far more, but with a startling level of grace. This ought to have put my own problems into proper scale. And for a few weeks it did, but eventually I started feeling sorry for myself, started self-dramatizing, started thinking that none of this would ever be over.

It wasn't the pain that did this, and it wasn't my anxiety about my condition. It was, I think, a growing sense of disconnection. Though I had a number of visits from friends during this time, I spent almost all of each day by myself. Granted, I'd spent a good part of each day by myself for months by then, and I'd never before had this sense of disconnection. The difference was that I was no longer reading.

As predicted, my "brain fog" had passed after a week on the antibiotics, so that I could read again, at least in the sense of making out the words. But it was difficult to concentrate long enough to do any serious reading. At any given moment, I was either under the sway of narcotics or incapable of thinking about anything except when I would next be allowed to fall back under their sway.

"I think that I cannot preserve my health and spirits," Thoreau wrote, "unless I spend four hours a day at least,—and it is commonly more than that,—sauntering through the woods and over the hills and fields."

Reading had become my way of sauntering, my way of being *sans terre*, at home in no one place but comfortable moving about the world, and it was these walks that I missed most. In all the time I'd been spending alone, I'd never felt lonely, because I had so many people to talk to. But now I had been shut away from them. I tried watching television, and it offered some distraction. But distraction was all it gave me, and once I wanted more, it became useless. Even the better shows weren't asking me to participate in a conversation.

In the days when I imagined myself becoming a writer like Montaigne or Thoreau, standing apart from society to read and write and think, I'd overlooked the fact that reading and writing are always ways of communicating with the world. Even if Thoreau's greatest pleasure was a long, solitary walk in the woods, he had to have the desire to convey this fact and its meaning to others, or to some part of himself that was in its own way a stranger, before attempting to write it down. He had to know that there were people out there who wanted to walk with him.

THE HARVARD CLASSICS

VERI
TAS

MONTAIGNE

September, or "Not of Athens, but of the World"

Volume XXIX: *The Voyage of the Beagle,* by Charles Darwin
Volume XXX: Scientific Papers
Volume XXXI: The *Autobiography* of Benvenuto Cellini
Volume XXXII: Literary and Philosophical Essays
Volume XXXIII: Voyages and Travels: Ancient and Modern
Volume XXXIV: *Discourse on Method,* by René Descartes
    Letters on the English, by Voltaire
    On Inequality among Mankind and *Profession of Faith of a*
        Savoyard Vicar, by Jean-Jacques Rousseau
    Of Man, Being the First Part of Leviathan, by Thomas Hobbes

When I told friends about my plan to read the Harvard Classics, most of them offered polite encouragement and left it at that. Among those who engaged a bit further, there was a certain consistency.

"How many books is that?" they would ask.

"There are fifty-one volumes," I'd tell them. "But some of them have two or three books, so it's more than a hundred."

They'd laugh.

"That sounds awful."

Then would follow some predictable joke about my desire to know more than everyone else, after which these friends would usually reveal more sincere skepticism, not about the idea itself, but about my ability to carry it out. Despite the frequency with which I heard this concern, it never seriously occurred to me that I wouldn't finish in time. I didn't say so to anyone, but I assumed that I could drop everything else in my life for a few months if necessary. But as the year progressed, I was reminded that life is full of things one can't simply drop. Also, there is no getting around waking up one morning to find that you can't read, that somewhere between your eyes and your brain the process of turning marks on a page into meaning has broken down.

After finishing those two volumes of essays during my weekend at the farm, I had thought that I was just about back on track with the Five-Foot Shelf. I didn't know that a month would pass before I could read another book. When I returned to the Shelf in early September, it seemed for the first time a real possibility that I might not finish within the year. What I had in front of me—twenty-three volumes, roughly ten thousand pages, to be read in four months—was perfectly feasible if everything else allowed, but the chance that everything else would allow seemed slimmer than ever.

Nor was the situation helped by the fact that my reentry was to come by way of *The Voyage of the Beagle* (1839). Darwin is the only writer to have two full volumes of the Harvard Classics dedicated to his work, and this fact must be a testament to his genius, and to his singular contribution to our understanding of humanity and how we came to be as we are. But this doesn't mean that I wanted to read another five hundred pages of him.

On the Origin of Species remained the most difficult volume I'd had to get through so far, and I had no reason to believe that *The Voyage of the Beagle* would be any better. In fact, *Voyage* is very different from what I expected; less like *On the Ori-*

gin of Species, more like *Two Years before the Mast*. It's the story of a young man going out to sea, and it begins much as you would expect such a story to begin. "After having been twice driven back by heavy southwestern gales," Darwin writes, "Her Majesty's ship Beagle, a ten-gun brig, under the command of Captain Fitz Roy, R. N., sailed from Devonport on the 27th of December, 1831."

On that day Darwin was two months shy of his twenty-third birthday. He had been until recently at Christ's College, Cambridge, which he'd entered after abandoning earlier studies in medicine. In preparation for entering the Anglican clergy, he had mostly studied theology at Cambridge, but he had also pursued his interest in natural history, geology, and entomology. When the time came for Darwin to take holy orders, a Cambridge don recommended him as a budding naturalist suitable to serve as a "gentleman's companion" on the *Beagle*'s expedition to survey Patagonia and Tierra del Fuego. Darwin's father was reluctant to allow him to go on a voyage, since that would delay his career in the Church, but the father acquiesced. The trip, expected to last two years, lasted almost five, and by the time it was done there was no question of Darwin's taking the cloth.

The Voyage of the Beagle gives scant attention to the details of seafaring, in part perhaps because Darwin didn't travel "before the mast" as Dana did, and in part because Darwin spent the vast majority of those years on land in South America. It was then that he began his careful observation of flora and fauna, which would set him on the path toward theories outlined more than twenty years later in *On the Origin of Species*. He also observed a great deal of human behavior, which makes for some of the book's most interesting material. He rode through the Argentine plains with gauchos, who taught him to throw a lasso. Some locals believed he possessed magic powers because of his compass and his watch; others seemed as worldly as Londoners.

Like Dana, Darwin left a modern city and encountered a considerably less settled world. He found some areas untouched by the West and others where colonialism and slavery had done their worst. At one point, he arrived on shore to discover that a revolution had broken out and the ports had been embargoed. "I found to my great surprise that I was to a certain degree a prisoner," he reports. The understated tone is typical; many of his observations about human life are offered with scientific detachment.

In some cases this tone can be rather troubling. He begins to sound like the narrator of a Conrad novel. "St. Fé is a quiet little town," he writes, "and is kept clean and in good order. The governor, Lopez, was a common soldier at the time of the revolution; but has now been seventeen years in power. This stability of government is owing to his tyrannical habits; for tyranny seems as yet better adapted to these countries than republicanism. The governor's favourite occupation is hunting Indians: a short time since he slaughtered forty-eight, and sold the children at the rate of three or four pounds apiece."

At another point, while describing a hunting expedition on which he is taken by a Portuguese priest, he writes, "We were accompanied by the son of a neighbouring farmer—a good specimen of a wild Brazilian youth. He was dressed in a tattered old shirt and trousers, and had his head uncovered: he carried an old-fashioned gun and a large knife. The habit of carrying the knife is universal; and in traversing a thick wood it is almost

necessary, on account of the creeping plants. The frequent occurrence of murder may be partly attributed to this habit."

I felt uneasy as I read those words—"specimen" and "wild"—
applied to this Brazilian boy. Human life seems to interest Darwin largely within the context of other concerns—the landscape,
plants, and animals. Indeed, Darwin's own writing often supports one of the chief objections made by evolution's opponents:
that the theory reduces human beings to the status of "mere"
animals. At times Darwin exhibits compassion for the native
peoples, but it is the same compassion he exhibits for a horse
suffering under a flogging.

"The scene on all sides showed desolation, brightened and
made palpable by a clear, unclouded sky," he writes upon arriv-
ing in Patagonia. "For a time such scenery is sublime, but this
feeling cannot last, and then it becomes uninteresting." He goes
on to tell a story, heard second hand, about his guide's brother,
who died in a storm. "His body was found two years afterward,"
Darwin notes, "lying by the side of his mule near the road, with
the bridle still in his hand." After continuing on to other stories
about entire parties being lost in similar circumstances, he concludes, "The union of a cloudless sky, low temperature, and a
furious gale of wind, must be, I should think, in all parts of the
world an unusual occurrence."

In this way, Darwin's interest in how a creature and its envi-
ronment interact seems to develop, over the course of the book,
from his own interaction with his strange new surroundings.
Watching these changes in the book's narrator is perhaps the
most exciting feature of *Voyage of the Beagle*. Darwin drew his
first book (as Dana did) directly from journals kept during his
trip, and he organized the book in journal form, so that it becomes, among other things, a record of his own intellectual

progress. Each passing month seems to change the way he observes his surroundings. By the time we reach the famous passages about the Galápagos archipelago, we are in the hands of a mature naturalist who takes us systematically through what he found there. Perhaps my own journey was having an effect, because I found these passages of minute observation far more interesting than their nearly identical counterparts in *On the Origin of Species*.

In his later writing, Darwin called his years with the *Beagle* the most important of his life. That time, he wrote, gave him the "habit of energetic industry and of concentrated attention to whatever I was engaged in, which I then acquired. Everything about which I thought or read was made to bear directly on what I had seen or was likely to see." The *Beagle* set off in 1831, just a few years before the *Pilgrim* left Boston Harbor with Richard Henry Dana aboard. In both cases, a journey that was seen at the time as a digression from a young man's charted path to adulthood proved instead to be formative: the very point, in fact, at which the man's true course in the world was set.

After finishing *The Voyage of the Beagle,* I thought a lot about traveling. Soon afterward, I read a volume dedicated to "Voyages and Travels," from Herodotus in Egypt to English explorers like Raleigh and Drake in the New World. It reminded me how much we have depended throughout history on a few people willing to go out into the world and then report on what they saw. Of course, there is a risk to all this secondhand knowledge. Herodotus was known as the "father of history," but also the "father of lies." Raleigh, too, took certain liberties: his essay "The Discovery of

Guiana" gives a largely fictionalized account of this opulent South American empire and its golden city, El Dorado. Not long after completing this account, Raleigh was imprisoned for almost fifteen years in the Tower of London, and it was during this time that he did most of his writing. By virtue of his descriptions of Guiana, he was freed to go back to El Dorado and claim it for the crown. But when this proved impossible, he was beheaded.

At about the time that I finished this volume of travels, my cousin Paul left for England. After his mother's death, Paul had applied to a graduate program in religion at Cambridge. He'd been accepted, and he had to decide whether to attend the program part-time or to leave his job at an accounting firm in New York and move away. He was in his early thirties, he had recently graduated from business school, and he worried that going back to school again might mean putting off his professional life. We all encouraged him to go. Though I didn't tell him as much, I thought about Darwin, who had also studied theology at Cambridge, and it seemed to me that this might be one of those digressive journeys that turn along the way into the path itself. Before Paul had even committed himself to attending the program full-time, Jim and I and my sister's husband Len were making plans to visit him in Cambridge as soon as possible.

The last time I'd left the country had been several years earlier, when my mother and I had taken a trip to Spain with Mimi, Paul, and Michael. In Madrid, we had stayed at a cheap hotel just off the Plaza Real, where the prostitutes grabbed at our pockets as we passed. Madrid is relatively small for a capital city; everything seemed to be within walking distance. One can spend weeks in Paris, London, or New York and still feel quite lost, but after only a few days we felt at home in Madrid. Each morning we went to a café in the plaza and had coffee. Then we walked across town to the Prado, the Reina Sofia, or the Museo Thyssen.

Mimi was a wonderful person to take to museums. She knew about art history, but when she spoke about a work of art, she spoke like a painter, noting strong brushstrokes here and the use of chiaroscuro there. She had a contagious sense of wonder, and I still remember standing beside her in silence before Picasso's *Guernica* and Goya's *Shootings of May 3rd*.

We had flown to Spain only a few weeks after the bombings at the Atocha station, and when we went there to catch a train to Barcelona, the station was filled with flowers and burning candles. Clearly, many people blamed the bombing on their government's support of the Iraq war, and we were occasionally mistreated when people discovered that we were American. In the train's dining car that day, we waited half an hour to have our order taken. It took us all that time, watching people who came in after us served in a matter of moments, to realize that there had been no oversight, that we were being ignored. Half-embarrassed, half-defiant, we returned to our seats.

But in Barcelona this was forgotten. We walked down the Ramblas to the beach, where we ate paella and drank wine. We went to the Antoni Gaudi park and later to the architect's great unfinished masterwork, the Sagrada Familia. I had bought Mimi a biography of Gaudi before we left, and standing before the cathedral she was able to recite to us the relevant facts about his life and work. (As I write now, the book remains on a shelf in her apartment, where her younger son Michael still lives.)

The cathedral is startling and strange in its design, but its scale is rather old-fashioned. To begin a project, to dedicate one's whole life to it as some workers did, knowing you will never live to see its completion—the beauty of this idea appealed to us all. The cathedral, which has been under construction since the late nineteenth century, is scheduled for completion in 2020. We agreed that we would come back together to see it when it was done. Mimi mentioned that she would be nearly eighty then, and we joked about wheeling her up into the massive central spire that one day will dominate the city's skyline but as of yet exists only in dreams.

I thought of traveling that month not only because I was reading about it, but because I was actually doing so little of it myself. I'd had two trips planned for August—one to North Carolina and one to Texas—but my illness forced me to cancel both. My best friend was getting married in Vermont later in the month, and I wasn't sure I would get to the wedding, either. I was in the midst of an intensive antibiotic regime for the Lyme disease while trying to rehabilitate my knee. The various doctors' offices and the hospital where I had my surgery were all within ten blocks of the apartment, which was a great convenience. But since my trips to these places were my only occasion to go outside, it also meant that for a hobbled month I remained within a half-mile radius.

Shortly after his return to England, Darwin suffered from an episode of heart palpitations. They were thought to be a result of overwork, but they proved instead to be the first symptoms of a chronic illness that stayed with him for the rest of his life. This illness was never properly diagnosed, but many people now speculate that it was caused by an insect bite suffered during his voyage. Now, Dr. Z warned me that he could make no assurances of a complete recovery. He asked me to keep a log of the improvement in my knee, giving the joint a letter grade each week. Once it had earned the same grade for several weeks in a row—whether an A or a D—it was likely to stay there.

It's a cliché to talk about reading as a journey, but it would be difficult to overstate how much easier my confinement became once I could read again. Throughout the year, I'd attempted to balance the Harvard Classics with the rest of my life. The two sides of the scale informed each other in surprising ways. Like Darwin, I felt that everything I read was made to bear on everything I saw. But now reading these books very nearly *was* my life. For weeks, I did almost nothing else.

While I read, I made notes about my journey, just as Dana and Darwin had done, though this being a different time, I posted mine on a blog. Even as I made my notes, I hoped they would become the foundation for this book. (I suspect that my predecessors had similar ideas, though neither admits as much.) Most of my notes were about the Classics themselves—summaries, brief stabs at literary criticism, efforts to put the works into context. I wrote little about the change I felt myself undergoing, though I was quite conscious of it. I had started reading for a number of reasons, and one of these was to put off making certain decisions. I hadn't intended to change my life, and I still remembered recoiling, months earlier, at writers like Franklin who seemed eager to impart practical knowledge. But as it happened, I took up this project at a time when I most needed what these books had to give me, and I gradually came to realize that I was being altered by these gifts. It was impossible to say—even now it is far too early to tell—how lasting the fruits of my journey might be, but the journey itself saw me safely through difficult times.

Between reading about Darwin's travels and reading about those of Herodotus and Raleigh, I came to the volume of "Literary and Philosophical Essays." The volume begins with Montaigne, who as I've said virtually invented the modern essay. At the age of thirty-five, after the death of his closest friend, he retired to his estates, where he wrote. He took his own personality, he said, as "the groundworke" of his book. Indeed, he is a kind of interior counterpart of Raleigh or Drake, an explorer of the self.

This isn't to say that the essays deal only with their author. Montaigne takes up all sorts of subjects—friendship, education, books, old age, death. But whatever topic he is ostensibly considering, he is always quick to warn his readers: "These are but my fantasies by which I endevour not to make things known, but my selfe."

Montaigne writes a great deal about the infirmity of the body and the prospect of mortality. "To philosophise," he states with beautiful bluntness in the title of one essay, "is to learne how to die." He explains that "studie and contemplation doth in some sort withdraw our soule from us"—that by thinking we are brought out of our bodies. For Montaigne, this drawing out is a preparation for death, when the soul and body will be forever severed. Though I didn't accept the religious implications that an infinite soul lives on after the finite body, I could easily recognize how "studie and contemplation" could draw one out of a feeble body, for this was exactly what was happening to me.

"When Socrates was demaunded whence he was," Montaigne writes in another essay, "he answered, not of Athens, but of the world; for he, who had his imagination more full and farther stretching, embraced all the world for his native Citie, and extended his acquaintance, his societie, and affections to all mankind: and not as we do, that looke no further than our feet."

This is a kind of precedent for Thoreau's Sainte-Terrer, the man at home anywhere his feet can take him. But here even one's feet aren't a limit. I read the rest of the essays in the collection with Montaigne in mind. Though I remained bedridden, I found my imagination growing fuller, stretching farther. I came upon other imaginations capable of bringing me out of myself. "For art has to leave reality," Friedrich Schiller writes in his "Letters upon the Aesthetic Education of Man" (1794). "It has to raise itself bodily above necessity and neediness; for art is the daughter of freedom, and it requires its prescriptions and rules to be furnished by the necessity of spirits and not by that of matter." And this is how I felt. Stuck in bed, with a throbbing knee that might never get better, but nonetheless free to read, I had been raised above necessity.

I wanted to believe that such freedom was always possible. I thought of Walter Raleigh in his prison tower, dreaming of El Dorado, a place half-discovered and half-invented (and perhaps hoping he'd never be sent out to find it). In the same way, as I lay in bed, I could set my book aside for a moment to think of Spain, to stand before the Sagrada Familia with a ghost. But just a few weeks earlier, this freedom had been completely un-available to me. I couldn't escape the knowledge that the body wins out in the end—or the knowledge that my own experi-ence was a trifle, tragedy replayed as farce, compared with what Mimi had gone through. In her last days, there was no possi-bility of imaginative escape. There was no attending to the necessities of the spirit, only to those of matter. What does one do with this fact?

Bound up in the typical objection to Darwinism—the objec-tion to seeing that Brazilian boy as a "wild specimen"—is the worry that seeing behavior as contingent on instinct and envi-ronment negates the possibility of free will. But doesn't this negation, pleasant or not, get at something unavoidable about our experience? We are subject to natural laws in whose legisla-tion and enforcement we have no say.

I've spent a fair amount of time over the past few years read-ing Immanuel Kant, which isn't exactly the same as saying that I've read a lot of him. The work is slow going, the syntax is tangled, the terms are obscure. But his great concerns—the limits of human knowledge, the battle between the ideal and the material, above all the effort to affirm human freedom in the face of physical determinism—fascinate me, so I return to his work periodically, usually with frustratingly little success. It is a kind of guilty pleasure. I say "guilty" because I'm gener-ally unable to give it the attention it deserves, and because Kant doesn't trade much with dabblers or dilettantes like me. I often suspect that if he could see me reading his work, he would ask me to stop.

But I reached a better understanding of Kant's ideas once I had finished his essay in this volume of the Classics. "Fundamental Principles of the Metaphysic of Morals" (1785) is a relatively early work that lays out in fairly direct terms the issues of moral philosophy that would occupy Kant for the rest of his life. No doubt this played a part in my increased understanding. But I think it was also because I was now better prepared for his ideas.

The mere fact that I was able to get through the essay indicated how far I'd come in the past weeks, both physically and mentally. Reading Kant is hard work. It would be impossible for me to render his argument in a satisfactory way without reproducing most of this long essay, but I will attempt a brief summary.

Kant begins by making a distinction between "material" knowledge and "formal" knowledge: "the former considers some object, the latter is concerned only with the form of the understanding and of the reason itself, and with the universal laws of thought in general without distinction of its objects." Formal knowledge, he explains, constitutes the philosophical branch of logic. He makes a further distinction between types of material knowledge, which can concern itself with objects subject to "the laws of nature or of freedom." He calls material knowledge of the laws of nature "physics." He calls knowledge of the laws of freedom "ethics." Finally, he calls the study of ethical laws "moral philosophy." (It is a common feature of Kant's writing that he begins by carefully defining his terms; one must keep his sometimes idiosyncratic definitions closely at hand.)

Leaving all these esoteric definitions behind, though, it may be enough to say this: Kant seeks to establish the existence of a world of freedom, parallel to but separate from the natural world. He recognizes that the physical world puts severe limits on our actions. Whether we are hungry, sick, or tired, whether we are able to get out of bed in the morning—these things may be out of our control. But there is another realm in which we are free. It is in this realm, he believes, that moral laws exist. This isn't an idea Kant expects his reader to take on faith. In fact, he spent much of his life carefully making his case. This essay provides a mere outline, and he would dedicate his career to filling it in. But even the outline is exhilarating. By the end of the essay, when Kant suggests that his work has approached "the very limit of human reason," any reader who has followed him this far will be inclined to agree.

The essay is an arduous but unforgettable journey, one I'm unequipped to reproduce here. I imagine that very few people outside academe undertake this journey, and I hesitate even to recommend it. I've never been one for the "take your medicine" school of culture. I read what I read, for the most part, because I like it. If I had enjoyed the television shows that I spent most of August watching, I would continue to watch them. But I didn't.

On the other hand, it isn't precisely enjoyment that one gets out of reading Kant. But neither is it practical knowledge. So why read him? Here I was reminded of Charles Eliot and his peers, and their idea that "culture" is more than the entertainment by which we're surround. Eliot took for granted that getting through the Classics would require hard work at times, but he knew that some readers would find this work worth doing—not because there was a reward at the end of it, but because the work itself was a reward. This is the feeling I had on finishing Kant's essay.

I can't see how it was "useful" from the evolutionary stand-point for Kant to dedicate his life to attempting to establish a basis for the legitimacy of moral laws that seem otherwise in-consistent with the demands of the physical world. Nor was it especially useful for me to spend several days attempting to understand his efforts. Nor for that matter can I see the evolu-tionary need for Darwin to develop his theories. This consid-eration does not imply that Darwin's theories are untrue; it just suggests that the theories may be imperfect tools for under-standing human experience.

When I finished this volume of essays, I thought back to a pas-sage I had read at the beginning of the year in Thomas Browne's *Religio Medici*. "Thus is Man that great and true *Amphibium*," Browne writes, "whose nature is disposed to live, not onely like other crea-tures in divers elements, but in divided and distinguished worlds: for though there be but one to sense, there are two to reason, the one visible, the other invisible."

The true *Amphibium*. Though I found this remark beautiful enough when I first read it, I didn't appreciate the impression it had made until it came back unbidden. Browne is speaking about the spiritual world, but one might just as easily think about Kant's realms of nature and freedom. That is, one need not believe in the spirit in any religious sense to accept that man, perhaps uniquely among animals, is capable of traveling in both the visible and the invisible worlds. It may be this fact above all others that separates the Brazilian boy from Darwin's other wild specimens.

Some people believe that we are this way because God made us so, others that rational thought is an evolved mechanism for survival. But one need not hold any opinion at all about how we came to be so. The fact is that we *are* so. In the end, the body may win out. Infirmity extends to the mind, it encroaches like a fog, and finally we are extinguished. But in the meantime, there is nowhere we can't go.

JEAN LOCKE

October, or "To My Own Sons, and Those of My Teachers"

It snowed on the day in the winter of my twenty-third year when my mother took me to spill my seed at the Empire State Building. The trip was an ex-girlfriend's idea.

"Have you thought about going to a sperm bank?" she had asked after hearing that I would be starting chemotherapy.

I was confused.

"What would I need sperm for?"

"Not to *withdraw*," she said delicately. "To deposit. So if your treatments cause any . . . damage, you'll have it for later."

I was still very much worried for my own life at that point, and I hadn't given any thought to my unconceived children.

"That might be a good idea," I allowed.

But in the days that followed I did nothing about it. A week later, she asked if I'd spoken with the doctor about our conversation. I told her that I hadn't.

"If you don't do it soon," she said, "it's going to be too late."

When I asked my oncologist at my next appointment, he confirmed that there was a possibility of complications in that area. In any case, he said, he didn't think it would be a good idea for me to try to have children for several years after finishing my treatments. I assured him that it wouldn't be an issue.

"But what about long-term?" I asked.

He considered judiciously.

"I don't expect there to be any permanent effect on your sperm count. But it's not unheard of. I can refer you to a place, if that would give you some peace of mind."

By the time I called the number on the card, it was too late to schedule an appointment until after my first chemotherapy session. I spoke with my oncologist, who said that any adverse effects would be unlikely to develop after just one treatment. I should go ahead and make the appointment, he added, if that's what I wanted.

This is how I came to be on my way to the Empire State Building, where the sperm bank was located. I went with my mother because, well, I went everywhere with my mother in those days. I couldn't get around by myself. My friends were back at school; my father was at work. My mother took me back and forth to school twice a week to attend the classes I had to keep up with in order to graduate in the spring. She took me to the oncologist's office once a week. She took me to all my medical appointments, and now she joined me at the sperm bank.

The front of the office was like any of the half dozen waiting rooms I'd visited in the preceding weeks. There was paperwork to fill out. I signed up for five years of storage, plus an additional fee for testing. Then I left my mother behind and headed down a long hallway to what looked like a high school biochemistry lab: there were beakers, vials, and lots of rubber gloves and white coats. A technician gave me a specimen cup and a roll of paper towels. Then she ushered me through a door. I'd like very much to pretend that what I found on the other side of that door was something other than a shopping mall changing room littered with well-worn copies of down-market pornography. Reader, I cannot.

Afterward, I returned to the waiting room, where my mother and I cracked a few jokes while we each stared intently at a distant spot over the other's shoulder, pretending that neither of us knew what I'd just been doing down the hall. Then we went home to prepare for whatever came next. These were the days when I was learning that something always came next.

★ ★ ★

Given my recent family history, I approached the medical writing in the Shelf with particular curiosity. The volume offers an odd but compelling picture of medical history. Predictably, it begins with Hippocrates. But the Hippocratic Oath and the Hippocratic Law (c. 460 BCE), like so much in the Classics, proved rather different from what I had expected. Granted, a few lines of their combined two and half pages are concerned with what we would now recognize as medical ethics. ("Into whatever houses I enter, I will go into them for the benefit of the sick, and will abstain from every voluntary act of mischief and corruption; and, further, from the seduction of females or males, of freemen and slaves.") But the primary concerns are the relationship between student and teacher, the passing on of the art, and initiation into the "mysteries of the science":

> I swear by Apollo the physician and Aesculapius, and Health, and All-heal, and all the gods and goddesses, that, according to my ability and judgment, I will keep this Oath and this stipulation—to reckon him who taught me this Art equally dear to me as my parents, to share my substance with him, and relieve his necessities if required; to look upon his offspring in the same footing as my own brothers, and to teach them this Art, if they shall wish to learn it, without fee or stipulation; and that by precept, lecture, and every other mode of instruction, I will impart a knowledge of the Art to my own sons, and those of my teachers, and to disciples bound by a stipulation and oath according to the law of medicine, but to none others.

Cleary, Hippocrates has a deep concern for the transmission and preservation of his esoteric knowledge. To his mind, such knowledge entails certain responsibilities, and it should not be wasted on those unwilling to accept these responsibilities. This is perhaps the most striking thing about the Hippocratic Oath— not that it binds the physician to pass on his art to worthy disciples, but that it binds him to withhold it from all others. The implication is that knowledge, gained at great cost, may be lost to humanity if not handled properly—that the ground in which it is planted must be properly cultivated, to use the metaphor Eliot and his colleagues liked so much.

Hippocrates came from a family of physicians said to be a descended from Aesculapius, the mythical god of medicine mentioned at the beginning of the oath. But this pedigree alone can't account for his emphasis on the family bonds that the knowledge creates, on the need to hold one's teachers "equally dear" as one's parents. It is as if knowledge is a family legacy, but— unusually—membership in the family is established by receipt of the legacy, rather than the other way around. In the proper order of things, each man has one teacher or father, but many students or children. And so the family grows over the generations. Because the legacy is carefully husbanded, because it is withheld from those who won't value it properly, it grows alongside the family.

In the weeks that followed, I thought very little about my visit to the Empire State Building. Years would pass before I might need the sperm I had deposited, if I ever needed it at all. Of course, I was glad to know it was there, if only because it allowed me to forget about an issue that had never held much urgency for me.

After a few more rounds of chemotherapy, I worried about little except forcing down food and keeping something close at hand to throw it up into. Then, as my condition improved, I returned to earlier concerns. Beyond my immediate health, these were finishing my senior thesis and getting to spend some time with my friends before we all graduated and scattered around the country. When people around me behaved too solemnly, or treated me too carefully, I sometimes told them about "going to the sperm bank with my mom"—a story that had the right amount of humor and awkwardness to keep them off balance.

Several months passed, and then a call came for me.

"Mr. Beha?" the woman asked.

"Yes?"

She introduced herself as calling from the sperm bank, whose name I didn't even recognize at first.

"We've completed the tests," she said, "and I'm afraid the specimens we took aren't viable."

"I don't understand," I told her.

"Were you suffering from an illness at the time you came to visit us?"

"Yes. I have Hodgkin's lymphoma."

"Are you being treated?"

"I had just started chemotherapy when I came in to see you."

"Either the disease itself or the treatment must have lowered your count."

"OK," I said. I waited for her to explain what this meant in practical terms.

"If you'd like us to destroy the remaining specimens, we can refund the storage costs."

"Do you think that's what I should do?"

"I'm afraid that they're not going to be much use to you in the future. The count is quite low, and in some cases the sperm are damaged."

"All right," I said. "I guess you should go ahead and destroy them."

She seemed to be relieved to have the matter settled.

"Great," she said. "I'll make that note on your file. Your Visa should be credited within two weeks."

I was surprised at how hurt I felt as I hung up the phone. I was twenty-two and single, and I had hardly given a thought to having children. I wouldn't even have taken the precaution of going to the sperm bank if others hadn't encouraged me. Besides, it might all have been unnecessary anyway—my doctors were hopeful that I would make a complete recovery, and that neither the illness nor its treatments would leave any permanent effects. So why did I feel bereft as I set down the receiver?

In retrospect, it seems odd that I should have thought so little about the prospect of children, because my sister Alice, who is just a year older than I am, had given birth to my nephew Peter just a few months earlier. Alice and her husband lived only minutes from the campus then, and while I was still at school full-time I saw them nearly every day. Now that I was going there only a few days each week, I made sure to see them as much as possible.

Would things have been different if I'd acted as soon as the idea of the sperm bank was suggested to me? Or was it already too late by then? Afterward, I felt as if I'd carelessly set aside something whose value I was only now coming to know.

*   *   *

In the event, Hippocrates was right to worry about the fate of his hard-earned knowledge. Like most Greek learning it was, if not lost, carelessly set aside for hundreds of years. The rest of the volume of medical writing represents in part the long effort to recoup that family legacy. After Hippocrates we jump almost two thousand years, to Ambroise Paré's *Journeys in Diverse Places* (1585). Paré was a barber-surgeon at a time when such practitioners were still carefully distinguished from physicians. (This distinction dates back at least to Hippocrates, who wrote, "I will not cut persons labouring under the stone, but will leave this to be done by men who are practitioners of this work.")

Paré's memoir of traveling with the French army—from 1537 in Turin to 1569 in Flanders—says far more about the state of warfare at the time than about any advances in medical knowledge. His work is mostly triage. "Now, as for the capture of Rouen," he writes in a typical passage, "they killed many of our men both before and at the attack: and the very next day after we had entered the town, I trepanned eight or nine of our men, who had been wounded with stones as they were on the breach. The air was so malignant, that many died, even of quite small wounds, so that some thought the bullets had been poisoned: and those within the town said the like of us; for though they had within the town all that was needful, yet all the same they died like those outside."

After Paré comes William Harvey, who in 1616 gave the lectures collected here as *On the Motion of the Heart and Blood in Animals*, in which he demonstrated human circulation. In making his case, he responds not to his peers or to the previous generation of doctors, but to the second-century Greek physician Galen, the first to argue that the veins, which empty themselves after death, are filled in the living not with air but with blood. Harvey writes as if no progress whatsoever has been made in this area in the intervening centuries. And so on, through the rest of the volume.

"It is characteristic of science," Louis Pasteur writes, "to reduce incessantly the number of unexplained phenomena." But as one reads, it seems that the great legacy lost in the centuries after Hippocrates and recovered by the modern era wasn't a body of knowledge as such, but a method for acquiring explanations from experience. In the first of his aphorisms (not included in the Classics), Hippocrates wrote, "Life is short, and Art long; the crisis fleeting; experience perilous, and decision difficult." In his essay about puerperal fever, Oliver Wendell Holmes quotes another doctor, who writes, "Those who have never made the experiment can have but a faint conception how difficult it is to obtain the exact truth respecting any occurrence in which feelings and interest are concerned." Holmes, Pasteur, Edward Jenner, Joseph Lister—each refers at length to experimental evidence to make his case. At the same time, most of them must also make a case for the value of experiment itself. They explain why received wisdom ought to be challenged.

The week before reading these medical writings, I read the volume of English philosophy containing John Locke, George Berkeley, and David Hume, the three leading figures in the modern school of empiricism. Locke, the movement's founder, was a doctor, but after studying medicine at Oxford, he spent most of his adult life as a tutor to the sons of a series of political and financial patrons. One of these patrons, Edward Clarke, asked him to set down his ideas about education, and the result was *Some Thoughts Concerning Education* (1693), which begins the thirty-seventh volume of the Harvard Classics.

There was a good deal of discussion about education going on in my family when I read this volume. After twenty years in school, from kindergarten to my master's degree, I had taught for a few semesters at the university where I went to graduate school. I had given up teaching now, and for the first time in many years the beginning of fall didn't bring a return to the classroom. Also, my sister had decided not send Peter back for his second year of school. She was going to educate her children herself.

I sometimes got looks from my friends when I told them my sister was homeschooling her children. I didn't blame them for their scepticism. There was a time when I might have been the one giving the looks. But my thoughts on the subject had changed, and I don't think it was merely in an effort to support my sister's decision. The Classics reminded me that our present education system, which we take for granted in so many ways, is a very new development. Far more common throughout history was the model described by Locke in *Some Thoughts Concerning Education*, in which a single tutor was assigned to handle all elements of a child's development —a system that echoes the "initiation" described by Hippocrates. By its nature, a tutorial system, with its one-on-one format, is incompatible with education for the masses, but that hardly seems a persuasive argument against its use by those in a position to use it.

"A sound mind in a sound body, is a short, but full description of a happy state in this world," Locke writes. "He that has these two, has little more to wish for; and he that wants either of them, will be but little the better for any thing else." For Locke, the goal of education isn't to transmit a set of facts but to cultivate this soundness, not just in mind, but in body. His view of education is so all-encompassing as to seem at times comical.

He begins with the child's dress (shoes and clothes should be thin, inuring the child against the cold) and moves on to environment (the child should spend as much time as possible out in the open air) and then to diet ("flesh should be forborne as long as he is in coats, or at least till he is two or three years old") and drink ("only small beer").

And then there is hygiene. Locke takes great interest in a child's bowel movements. "People that are very loose," he writes, "have seldom strong thoughts, or strong bodies." As the same time, "costiveness has too its ill effects." Locke's solution to this problem is that the child should be sent to "make court to Madam Cloacina" at the same time each morning, whether he wants to or not, until the habit is fixed.

"Due care being had to keep the body in strength and vigour, so that it may be able to obey and execute the orders of the mind," he goes on, "the next and principal business is, to set the mind right, that on all occasions it may be dispos'd to consent to nothing but what may be suitable to the dignity and excellency of a rational creature."

When it comes to setting the mind right, Locke explains, the four requisites of a rational creature are virtue, wisdom, breeding, and learning. Note that learning comes last among these; the vast majority of Locke's work is dedicated to the first three attributes. To achieve them, the first habit that must be instilled

is self-denial. "It seems plain to me," he writes, "that the principle of all virtue and excellency lies in a power of denying ourselves the satisfaction of our own desires, where reason does not
authorize them."

Eventually, Locke does arrive at the more typical subjects of
education, but he makes no apologies for their place among his
priorities:

> You will wonder, perhaps, that I put learning last, especially
> if I tell you I think it the least part. This may seem strange in
> the mouth of a bookish man; and this making usually the
> chief, if not only bustle and stir about children, this being
> almost that alone which is thought on, when people talk of
> education, makes it the greater paradox. . . . Learning must
> be had, but in the second place, as subservient only to greater
> qualities. Seek out somebody that may know how discreetly
> to frame his manners: place him in hands where you may, as
> much as possible, secure his innocence, cherish and nurse up
> the good, and gently correct and weed out any bad inclina-
> tions, and settle in him good habits. This is the main point,
> and this being provided for, learning may be had into the
> bargain, and that, as I think, at a very easy rate, by methods
> that may be thought on.

From here, Locke's curriculum is fairly straightforward. He
begins with reading and writing, first in English and then in
French and the classical languages. He moves on to geometry
and algebra, then to history and sciences. But the subjects are
almost beside the point. The real work—forming a sound mind
in a sound body—is done before we even arrive at "learning."
Underlying all of Locke's efforts is the assumption that the

child begins as a tabula rasa, that lifelong attributes can be constructed as if from scratch in the earliest years of life. Locke believes in the ultimate malleability of the child. He writes, "I imagine the minds of children as easily turn'd this or that way, as water it self."

We tend now to believe that a good deal of who we are is genetic, that what we inherit from our parents at conception determines much of who we will become. Set beside this idea, Locke's view comes to look more like that of Hippocrates: our education is our true family legacy; it initiates us into bonds that can be more meaningful than biology. And the purpose of this education is to form us into a certain kind of person.

As the year progressed, and I neared the end of this reading project, people often asked me what I had learned from the Classics. Mostly, they wanted to be told trivia and unusual facts. Occasionally I had a good answer to give them. From William Harrison's *Description of Elizabethan England* (1577), I had learned of the "several disorders and degrees amongst our idle vagabonds." It made a neat party trick to list Harrison's terms—rufflers, uprightmen, bawdy-baskets. But more often my mind turned embarrassingly blank in response to this question. I couldn't possibly tell the truth, which was that I had a growing sense of being initiated into the mysteries of a kind of fraternity. I couldn't even tell people the slightly less pretentious truth that I was learning more about how to be in the world than I was any particular facts or figures. Part of the nature of the "internal cultivation" that Eliot and his precursors held dear is that it doesn't display itself to others. It isn't a status symbol, and it won't change your social standing. Because it is a process rather than a final outcome, it can't even really be explained.

★   ★   ★

It wasn't actually the volume of medical writing that put me in mind of my visit to the sperm bank and the aftermath of that visit. I came to see the works contained in the Classics as a cultural legacy, and wondered what losing that legacy would mean. I thought of my grandmother reading these books. How had they affected what she taught her daughters? Had they in turn passed these lessons on to me and my brother and sister and cousins, without any of us really understanding their source?

Near the end of the month, I got a chance to go to Alice's house during the week, and to see the family's school day. The curriculum was about what Locke might have suggested for a child of Peter's age—mostly reading and writing, with some basic arithmetic. But education wasn't set apart from the rest of life. It was of a piece with learning to brush one's teeth and to show the proper manners at meals. Peter's younger siblings were engaged in these lessons, too, just as they spent the "school" time with shapes, colors, and stories. As in most contemporary homeschooling contexts, religion is very important in my sister's home, so school lessons were incorporated naturally with morning and evening prayers and lessons from the Bible. As much weight was given to the first three of Locke's requisites—wisdom, virtue, and breeding—as to the last.

Though I'm in my fifth year of remission, entering the period when one begins to think of oneself as "cured," I don't know what the long-term effects of my cancer or its treatments will be. I've made no effort to find out whether my "count" has returned to normal, and I don't plan on finding out soon.

The issue does come to mind once in a while, and I'm sure that it will become more pressing in coming years. But as I sat in the dining room—the classroom—with my nieces and nephews, it seemed to me that the things my sister was teaching them, and not any accidents of biology, made them her children.

November, or "Food for Future Years"

My father's father loved poetry. Whenever we came to visit, he would recite to us at the dinner table. He was a great fan of nonsense rhymes—

> One dark day in the middle of the night,
> Two dead boys got up to fight.
> Back-to-back they faced each other,
> Drew their swords and shot each other.

—but also of Coleridge and Tennyson. He had no time for modernism, for T. S. Eliot, Wallace Stevens, or William Carlos Williams; and he didn't follow the fashions of contemporary poetry. In fact, he preferred nothing more recent than Longfellow, the last truly popular poet in the English language, whose "The Village Blacksmith" and "Paul Revere's Ride" were particular favorites of his. It might be said that he loved *verse*, rather than poetry as such: if a poem didn't rhyme or at least have a fairly regular meter, it didn't seem to interest him. But he mixed high and low with the ease of a committed postmodernist, so that "It is an ancient Mariner, / And he stoppeth one of three" could be shortly followed by a few lines from "Yes, We Have No Bananas."

My grandfather was a well-educated man, but he wasn't especially literary. During summers at the Farm, he read Dick Francis mysteries. At home his shelves were mostly filled with historical books, especially books about the area in upstate New York where our family had settled. Although he occasionally took down and read from his *Treasury of Best-Loved Poems*, he seemed to have had a fixed store of verses memorized for longer than I could remember, and I never noticed any new works being added to this store over time. But what he knew he knew well: later in his life, when his short-term memory was failing, he could still recite those lines. I imagine that these fragments of poems were for him rather like certain lines from *Caddyshack* or *Fletch* for me, lines that my friends and I had all absorbed in childhood and could reproduce at any time, even if we hadn't watched the movies in years.

Once or twice while I read the Classics I played with the thought that my approach was precisely backward: I ought to have chosen just one book to read that year and dedicated myself to it until I knew it perfectly. This was mostly a passing fancy. More persistent and serious were my doubts about having set arbitrary deadlines to get through books that deserved however much time they demanded. Why limit oneself to a week for all of Milton's poems or Emerson's essays, when a single work by either man might have occupied months? The absurdity of my plan stuck in the back of

my mind throughout the year. Most of the time it seemed necessary, or at least excusable. After all, there is some value to breadth
as well as depth. But there were moments when my rush through
the Classics seemed inexcusable.

This feeling was particularly acute during the last week of
October and the first week of November, as I read the three
volumes of English and American poetry. Eliot and Neilson
appropriated these volumes—1,508 pages in all—from an existing anthology, probably something much like the treasuries from
which my grandfather first learned "Ozymandias" and "The
Rime of the Ancient Mariner." Neilson made a few adjustments,
cutting out Milton and Burns, each of whom already had a volume of his own, and adding a few others. Otherwise, the anthology was absorbed in its entirety.

I enjoyed these poems as much as anything in the Classics,
but that was precisely the problem: every few pages I came to a
poem that I wanted to linger over for hours or days. If I could
have changed one thing about my approach, I decided during
those weeks, it would have been this: I would have separated
those three volumes from the rest and read them bit by bit
throughout the year. I might have set aside time for two or three
poems a day, allowing myself a full evening for the better ones.
I could have spent a week or two with the very best, staying with
each until it was memorized, as my grandfather must have done.
As it was, I couldn't take my time if I wanted to finish on schedule. So I pressed on, turning the pages like those of a novel or a
biography, knowing all the while that poetry—especially the
short lyric poetry that dominates the English tradition—isn't
meant to be read in this way.

About halfway through the second of these three volumes, I
came to William Wordsworth's "Tintern Abbey." (Its full title is

more of a mouthful: "Composed a Few Miles above Tintern Abbey, on Revisiting the Banks of the Wye during a Tour July 13, 1798.") I'd read the poem, which is among Wordsworth's best and most famous, a few times before, both in high school and in college.

The abbey itself, which was abandoned in the sixteenth century, still stands in ruins near the Wye River in the Welsh countryside. When Wordsworth visited the area on the occasion of this poem, he was returning for the first time since 1793:

> Five years have past; five summers, with the length
> Of five long winters! and again I hear
> These waters, rolling from their mountain-springs
> With a soft inland murmur.

For several lines after this, Wordsworth describes the landscape around the abbey, which remains mostly unchanged, so that he is really describing both visits at once: "Once again I see / These hedge-rows, hardly hedge-rows, little lines / Of sportive wood run wild." But then there is a shift, from these two moments in time as they reflect each other to the years that stretched between them. Throughout those years, we learn, this landscape remained present to Wordsworth (or to "the speaker," as a more academic reader would surely insist). "These beauteous forms, / Through a long absence, have not been to me / As is a landscape to a blind man's eye." He explains that he has often turned to his memories of these "forms" while stuck amid "the din / Of towns and cities." There, "in hours of weariness," they have offered him relief. But this isn't all. In lines that are among his best known, Wordsworth attempts to describe the full extent of his debt:

To them I may have owed another gift,
Of aspect more sublime; that blessed mood,
In which the burthen of the mystery,
In which the heavy and the weary weight
Of all this unintelligible world,
Is lightened:—that serene and blessed mood,
In which the affections gently lead us on,—
Until, the breath of this corporeal frame
And even the motion of our human blood
Almost suspended, we are laid asleep
In body, and become a living soul:
While with an eye made quiet by the power
Of harmony, and the deep power of joy,
We see into the life of things.

With an eye made quiet . . . we see into the life of things. Wordsworth might have ended here, and we would have been left
with something beautiful. But he presses on. The appreciation
of the profound gifts that his first visit to this spot has given
him over the years leads to a new realization, that one day he
will be able to rely for similar comfort on the moment he is
now experiencing, "that in this moment there is life and food/
For future years."

Whereas the earlier descriptions of an unchanging landscape had collapsed time, folding five years into a single view,
this development in the poem stretches time out. As it does,
Wordsworth is forced to recognize that, although much remains
the same about the landscape, his relationship to it has changed.
His pleasure is no longer as simple, nor as immediate. But with
this loss has come "abundant recompense":

> For I have learned
> To look on nature, not as in the hour
> Of thoughtless youth; but hearing oftentimes
> The still, sad music of humanity,
> Nor harsh nor grating, though of ample power
> To chasten and subdue.

We have arrived at a second point where Wordsworth might comfortably have ended the poem. But once again he pushes on. For the first time, he mentions his companion on this tour, his younger sister Dorothy, whom he now addresses directly. He sees in her reaction the direct, youthful passion that he once possessed. He knows this state can't last for her any more than it has lasted for him, so he wishes that her relationship to nature will evolve in the same way as his own. He ends by urging her—while also urging himself—to remember,

> That on the banks of this delightful stream
> We stood together; and that I, so long
> A worshipper of Nature, hither came
> Unwearied in that service . . .
> Nor wilt thou then forget,
> That after many wanderings, many years
> Of absence, these steep woods and lofty cliffs,
> And this green pastoral landscape, were to me
> More dear, both for themselves and for thy sake!

I love the ambiguity of "we," which can refer either to Wordsworth and his sister or to Wordsworth and his younger self. And "unwearied" at once echoes and contradicts the earlier "hours of weariness." I also love how the movement of attention from his years of absence back to the landscape reverses the process at the poem's beginning.

If I've labored my reading here, it's perhaps because I've given more attention to these four pages than to any others in the Classics. Just as John Stuart Mill once did, I came to Wordsworth in the midst of a difficult period, when the pleasures of life felt dull to me. And, like Mill, I had not gone to Wordsworth to solve this problem. I'd merely stumbled on him. When I came across these pages in early November, in the midst of several hundred other poems, I stopped what I was doing. The poem had an overwhelming effect on me, and I didn't want to leave it until I had figured out why.

As it happens, it had been a little over five years—"five summers, with the length of five long winters"—since I'd last read "Tintern Abbey." For the sake of symmetry, I'd like to say that I was as moved by the poem as Wordsworth had been by his earlier trip to the banks of the Wye, that I'd kept its words with me all that time, and that they had lifted me from weariness. But it isn't true. My earlier response had been mostly academic. This was not surprising, perhaps: I'd read it in preparation for my senior comps.

I wasn't a good student in college. I didn't care what grades I got, so I read what interested me—mostly contemporary fiction—and didn't worry about the rest. But by the end of my senior year, I had decided to apply to graduate school, and so my grades became a more pressing issue. My cancer treatments didn't allow for the usual senior spring shenanigans, but I was far enough along in my recovery to have a certain amount of restless energy. I was no longer too sick to get around by myself, and I was once again spending the week on campus. So I studied. Over the course of a few weeks, I reread (or in many cases read for the first time) most of the introductory English literature syllabus.

This was a pleasure rather than a chore. I've always been fascinated with figuring out how pieces of literature *work*, and this is basically how I approached those weeks. I tried to be a careful and attentive reader. Much of what I've just written about "Tintern Abbey" I could have put into a blue book then if asked. (As it happens, I wasn't asked, and I didn't do particularly well on the test.) I appreciated the workings of the poem at the time, but I wasn't really moved by it. I never quite understood why certain professors had a wild look in their eyes when they spoke about the English Romantics.

But when I returned to "Tintern Abbey" five years later, my response was different. What I admired about the poem now was its picture of lost innocence leading to enrichment of experience. Not that Wordsworth denied the loss, but he appreciated the "abundant recompense" which might be offered in return. Like the poet himself, I felt more attuned now to the passage of time than I had during my last visit to "Tintern Abbey." And just as he imagined the future, when his memory of that place would give him pleasure, so I now hoped that his poem, or at least some part of it, would stay with me.

Though none of this was sufficient to explain the depth of my response, I had by then spent several days reading and thinking about this poem, and I had to move on. I made my way through the rest of that volume and then through the next, which includes Tennyson, Longfellow, and many of the poems my grandfather loved so much. After the poetry came "American Historical Documents." In its way, this volume was just as much of a revelation as Wordsworth's poem.

Any set of "great books" assumes to some degree that history can be transmitted through primary sources. Instead of an essay about the Enlightenment, you read Locke and Rousseau. Instead of a study of the Italian Renaissance, you read the *Autobiography* of Benvenuto Cellini. As a result of this principle, the few historians who are included in the Harvard Classics must be smuggled in under other guises. Thus, Herodotus and Tacitus become travel writers, and the *Chronicles* of Jean Froissart becomes a kind of romance, placed beside Thomas Malory's *Morte D'Arthur*.

In this spirit, American history is approached by way of a series of documents, beginning with an account of Leif Ericson's voyage to Vinland and ending with the convention between the United States and Panama for the completion of the Panama Canal, signed just a few years before the Harvard Classics appeared. In between are all the usual documents—the Mayflower Compact, the Declaration of Independence, the Constitution, the Emancipation Proclamation. There are also less familiar examples, like the Massachusetts Body of Liberties. And then there are all the treaties by which the manifest destiny of a small sliver of Atlantic coastline was achieved. (On the basis of these latter documents, one would be forgiven for thinking that the United States has done little throughout its short history but engage in wars of acquisition.)

It could be argued that this approach gives us history unfiltered, without the historian's interpretation. This sense of an immediate relationship to the past is one of the Shelf's greatest pleasures. But of course there has been, and must be, a filter—not every document can be included. In that sense, this one volume is a microcosm of the Classics as a whole: by deciding what's in and what's out, the editors shape a story about our past, even if that story is told entirely in other people's words. The synthesizing historian also shapes a story, but if he's any good he admits as much and makes a case for why his story is better than all the other stories he might as easily have built from the same materials. In a primary source, on the other hand, we have only what's included, without even the shadow of what's been left out.

The use of primary sources has other risks. A history told in treaties is almost by definition a history written by the winners, who tend to set the terms for a cease-fire. Throughout history the majority of people couldn't even read such documents, let alone write them, so the public record tends to give the masses short shrift. But the greatest risk, for the common reader at least, seems to be boredom. The job of the popular historian isn't just to sort and sift, but to make the raw material of history come alive. And so the big surprise of this volume, filled mostly with political documents, is how wonderfully alive it actually is. In fact, that it makes the language of contemporary public life look depressingly dead by comparison.

We already know that this is true of the Declaration of Independence, *The Federalist,* and Washington's Farewell Address. We understand that these works reach heights of both beauty and intelligence that our contemporary political discourse would never attempt. But we tell ourselves that history happens to have gathered together at that time and place a number of political geniuses —Jefferson, Hamilton, Madison,

Jay—who also happened to be literary geniuses. Alongside these works stand Lincoln's first Inaugural Address, his Gettysburg Address, and his letter to Mrs. Bixby, the Bostonian woman who lost five sons in the Civil War, to whom he wrote, "I pray that our Heavenly Father may assuage the anguish of your bereavement, and leave you only the cherished memory of the loved and lost, and the solemn pride that must be yours to have laid so costly a sacrifice upon the altar of freedom." Again, we tell ourselves that Lincoln was a man of a particular genius. Not every generation is afforded such a man, and it is no great shame that ours has none.

All this is fair enough. But what are we to make of Frank Haskell?

Frank Aretas Haskell was a lieutenant in the Union Army. He fought at Gettysburg, and he wrote an account of the battle that is startling in its honest beauty. "The great battle of Gettysburg is now an event of the past," it begins. "The composition and strength of the armies, their leaders, the strategy, the tactics, the result, of that field are today by the side of those of Waterloo— matters of history. A few days ago these things were otherwise." Haskell is wise here in his recognition of the way that time closes the door irrevocably behind us, so that the chaos of the immediate past becomes frozen in historic inevitability. A few lines later, he describes "the Rebel": "he was flushed with recent victory, was arrogant in his career of unopposed invasion, at a favorable season of the year."

Haskell offers this description of the Union soldiers marching toward the battlefield.

Onward they moved—night and day were blended—over many a weary mile, through dust, and through mud, in the broiling sunshine, in the flooding rain, over steeps, through defiles, across rivers, over last year's battle fields, where the skeletons of our dead brethren, by hundreds, lay bare and bleaching, weary, without sleep for days, tormented with the newspapers, and their rumors, that the enemy was in Philadelphia, in Baltimore, in all places where he was not, yet these men could still be relied upon, I believe, when the day of conflict should come. "Haec olim meminisse juvabit." We did not then know this.

(Before going any further, I'll admit that it took Google to tell me that *Haec olim meminisse juvabit* comes from Virgil: "Perhaps some day we will look fondly on all this," Aeneas tells his troops before setting off for Italy.)

Haskell maintains this tone throughout another hundred pages, during which he describes three days of battle that left 40,000 Confederate soldiers and 23,000 Union soldiers dead or wounded. Among the wounded was Haskell himself. Though he obviously sides with the Union, he adds that, "the enemy, too, showed a determination and valor worthy of a better cause. Their conduct in this battle even makes me proud of them as Americans."

After all that, he reaches for a new rhetorical height, closing with this flourish:

Another spring shall green these trampled slopes, and flowers, planted by unseen hands, shall bloom upon these graves; another autumn and the yellow harvest shall ripen there—all not in less, but in higher perfection for this poured out blood. In another decade of years, in another century, or age, we hope that the Union, by the same means, may repose in a securer peace and bloom in a higher civilization. Then what matters it if lame Tradition glean on this field and hand down her garbled sheaf—if deft story with furtive fingers plait her ballad wreaths, deeds of her heroes here? or if stately history fill as she list her arbitrary tablet, the sounding record of this fight? Tradition, story, history—all will not efface the true, grand epic of Gettysburg.

Every war produces its literary masters. No doubt there are men and women in Iraq or Afghanistan right now who will return home and write moving and beautiful books that attempt to make sense of the experience. But Haskell never returned home; he died in battle less than a year after Gettysburg. And he wasn't a budding young writer when he served; he was a lawyer in his thirties, commissioned into his local militia. His account is contained in a letter written to his brother and never intended for publication.

A number of other works in the Classics, ostensibly at least, weren't written for publication, beginning with Woolman's journals in the first volume. But of all these, Haskell's writing seems purest. It's just a letter home—a letter home that quotes Virgil in the original Latin, casually alludes to at least half a dozen other poets, and ends on a note that is at once impossibly elevated and still pitch-perfect.

Most men on the battlefield at Gettysburg, or any other battlefield throughout history, couldn't possibly have written this letter. A good many of them couldn't write at all. But Haskell's talent—not the talent of the professional writer, but the talent of the man who has seen something powerful and possesses the means to express it to others—hardly seems to exist anymore. These days there might be a news photographer embedded with those troops, and his images would be sent around the world before the battle was even over. We would find them on a Web site or attached to an e-mail and think that we were seeing what really happened. But when Haskell's letter is placed beside the speeches of Washington and Lincoln, and the writings of Jefferson, Madison, and Jay, all of them soldiers, politicians, or jurists first and writers next, it's difficult to avoid the conclusion that we have lost a collective ability for self-expression.

This conclusion seemed evident to me when I finished Haskell's letter, but it's possible that I never would have come to it had I not still been reading Wordsworth. I had returned to him several times that week, going over his poem every day or two to consider its effect on me.

At the time when Wordsworth published "Tintern Abbey," his work was considered shockingly unpoetic. In fact, he was impelled to defend his use of language in his preface to *Lyrical Ballads* (1798), the early collection of his and Coleridge's work in which "Tintern Abbey" appeared. This defense is included in the Classics' volume of "Prefaces and Prologues," which I read in late October, the week before I started reading the poetry.

His poems, Wordsworth tells us, "were written chiefly with a view to ascertain how far the language of conversation in the middle and lower classes of society is adapted to the purposes of poetic pleasure." He warns that readers who are used to the "gaudiness and inane phraseology of many modern writers" may find his work strange or awkward: "they will look round for poetry, and will be induced to inquire by what species of courtesy these attempts can be permitted to assume that title."

It would surprise most readers now to hear Wordsworth's description of his own language after reading about "that blessed mood, / In which the burthen of the mystery, / In which the heavy and the weary weight / Of all this unintelligible world, / Is lightened." It's not just the relative elegance of his supposed "awkwardness" that is so striking, but the complexity of this "language of conversation."

One could be charitable and say that colloquial language evolves over time, that what seems conversational in one era is destined to sound strange more than a century later. But this won't quite do. Wordsworth's conversational language isn't just different from ours; it's richer and more beautiful. Simply put, something has been lost. When I came to this conclusion, I thought back to my grandfather. It seemed to me that our decline in self-expression rested somewhere in the fact that he had grown up memorizing lines from Longfellow whereas I had grown up memorizing lines from *Caddyshack*.

I thought very little throughout the year about the marginalization of classic literature or what this marginalization might mean. I hadn't started reading the Classics to prove any grand point, and I wasn't interested in firing a shot in a culture war that was as much a part of history now as Gettysburg or Waterloo. I was reading for myself.

But now that the end of the year approached, I wondered what would happen to my reading life—and, in fact, to my life in general—after I was done with the Shelf. Of course, I would still read a fair amount, as I have done for as long as I've known how. But what would I read? Putting down the volume of American documents to revisit "Tintern Abbey" marked the first time

all year that I had gone back over a work in the Shelf after setting it aside. This simple act brought a wonderful revelation: that
I could relive these poems—or any of these books—whenever I
wanted.

It must seem an odd thing for one to "realize" about books
at such a late stage in the game. But somewhere in my months
of checking titles off a list I had forgotten the simple fact that
great books were meant to be reread. In many ways, this is precisely what makes them great. It felt invigorating to be reminded
of this truth, to be reminded that I could live with these books
for as long as I wanted, that I never had to return to the cultural
landscape I'd left behind for most of this year.

But a certain sadness came with this realization. After all, one
wants to go home. One wants—at least, I want—to be part of a
shared conversation. It is one thing to spend a brief time cut off
from popular culture, reading books that most of your acquain-
tances will never open. It's quite another to spend the rest of
your life traveling by way of signposts invisible to your own
friends, while their signposts remain invisible to you. If I was
going to spend the rest of my life with these books, then I needed
to have a greater stake in their fate in the world.

I was forced then to reconcile myself to the fact that Wordsworth and his cohort aren't relevant anymore, in the way that
even the worst television show remains relevant so long as it
avoids being canceled. And though I had no interest in being a
scold, I was also forced to recognize that this state of affairs had
cost us something. We are no longer able to make ourselves
known to each other, or perhaps even to ourselves, in the way
that we once were.

★   ★   ★

My thinking about all this was complicated the following week, when I moved on to the two volumes of "sacred writing." These volumes include the Analects of Confucius as well as passages from the Koran and from Hindu scripture. But their bulk consists of passages from the Hebrew Bible (Job, Psalms, and Ecclesiastes) and the New Testement (Luke, Acts, and the First and Second Letters to the Corinthians). I had read all these works before, and I had heard certain passages of them countless times during Mass while growing up. I still knew them well. And when I reread these works, I recognized them as the true literary connection between Washington and Lincoln and Haskell (and, for that matter, my own grandfather). Even the atheist Jefferson made his own version of the Gospels, cutting out all the miracles, omitting any hint of the supernatural, and leaving only the teachings of Jesus.

I have mentioned that in addition to the Classics, my maternal grandmother's shelves were mostly filled with works on Catholicism. My father's parents, too, had countless religious books on their shelves. Today, it often seems that we are split between the forces of "faith" (mostly in the middle of the country) and the forces of "culture" (mostly on the coasts). But I'm often struck by the degree to which religion *was* culture for both sides of my family. This is something that Charles Eliot and his peers would have taken for granted. They believed in culture as a means of moral development, and religion was a central element of this cultivation. In their case, religion meant a benign, vague sort of Unitarianism, but the number of books in the Shelf that relate to religion in all its varieties is likely to startle a modern, secular reader. Even those authors, like Hobbes or Darwin, who argue against spiritual faith understand without question that they must grapple with it. All this being so, how strong a position could

I possibly take on the culture of the past and the tragedy of its disappearance, when I had chosen to stand apart from a religious tradition that is central to that culture?

Here is where the wild-eyed literature professor would point out that Wordsworth's great moments of revelation came not at Tintern Abbey but "a few miles" from it. The professor would add that the abbey itself was already in ruins before Wordsworth got there. If Wordsworth understood that modern life seems to leave us little room for the sublime, he also understood that reconnecting to that force was no longer so simple as walking back into the abbey.

The more honestly I considered the complexity of the problem, the better I understood why the poem had grabbed me and wouldn't let go. I also came to a fuller answer to the ever-present question of why, exactly, I was reading the Classics in the first place. I wanted to establish a connection with those who came before me, even if I couldn't accept the faith that was central to their lives. I wanted to believe that for all the things lost, there might be abundant recompense somewhere.

My mother was the hostess at Thanksgiving, and members of both sides of my family came to the apartment to sit down at the table together. My sister's kids ran around as they tend to do, like tops that have been wound up with no particular destination in mind. I wondered if any of them would read Longfellow or Wordsworth when they were my age. I imagined a Thanksgiving dinner a few years from now, when, a propos of nothing, I would recite, "These hedge-rows, hardly hedge-rows, little lines / Of sportive wood run wild." I imagined my nephew, a teenager by then, rolling his eyes at me. I thought of the joy in my grandfather's face as he told us that "In Xanadu did Kubla Khan / A stately pleasure-dome decree." He didn't seem to worry about whether we understood his words or knew from where they came, as if in the end he was really speaking not to us but to himself, reminding himself that he carried these words within him, this food for future years.

THE HARVARD CLASSICS

VERI
TAS

PASCAL

December, or "The Thinking Reed"

In the first week of December, I flew to England with my brother Jim, my brother-in-law Len, and Len's brother, J.P. My cousin Paul had finished his first term at Cambridge, and we were going to visit him. While most of the cabin was plugged into the in-flight entertainment—Nicole Kidman in a remake of *Invasion of the Body Snatchers*—I read the second of two volumes of Elizabethan drama. I'd finished the first volume, Shakespeare and Marlowe, a few days earlier.

There is so much to be said about Shakespeare that I'm tempted to say nothing at all. Of the four or five very best imaginative writers in our history, only Shakespeare wrote in English. The other writers of his caliber—Homer and Dante, certainly; perhaps also Virgil and Cervantes—are represented in the Harvard Classics by mostly indifferent translations. This leaves the volume containing *Hamlet, Lear, Macbeth,* and *The Tempest* as the unquestionable literary high point of the Shelf.

It was a bit jarring to look around at a rapt, though admittedly captive, audience of passengers wearing headphones and be reminded that Shakespeare's plays were once the most popular of mass entertainments. This was true not just in Elizabethan England, but in nineteenth-century America, when Shakespeare was performed consistently in theaters throughout the country. These theaters drew not a "highbrow" audience, but the typical heterogeneous mix drawn by blockbuster movies today.

This state of affairs was changing by the time the Classics appeared, but Shakespeare's work was still so widely available that Collier tried to keep him off the Shelf for this reason. And when Eliot's partial list found its way to the press, Shakespeare's absence from it was the first thing remarked upon. Of course, Shakespeare is still one of the first names that come to mind when people think of the "classics," but there is something forbidding about him to many. In the nineteenth century—when Longfellow or Mark Twain could fill huge lecture halls throughout the country—scenes from Shakespeare were performed in small mining outposts and in front of crowds of prospectors above a saloon in San Francisco. These scenes were interspersed with contemporary songs, gymnastics, and minstrel shows.

Actually, the growing reverence for these plays brought a sense that they shouldn't be mixed with trifling entertainments, and this attitude precipitated the decline in Shakespeare's mass appeal. Nobody benefits by the process through which the best of what is popular is separated out, "purified," until it is no longer popular. But as the companion volume of Elizabethan and Jacobean drama in the Classics suggests, Shakespeare's greatest tragedies began standing more or less comfortably beside largely disposable work.

I don't mean to suggest that, say, Thomas Dekker's plays are bad. They're entertaining enough. I wouldn't walk out of a performance of one feeling cheated. But they don't compare to Shakespeare any better than anything else does. The other plays in this volume serve as a reminder that unlike Wordsworth's "lower class conversation," Shakespeare's language hasn't been made strange by the distance of time. It was always strange. Perhaps we once had a larger appetite for such strangeness.

Here is the beginning of "The First Three-Men's Song," from Dekker's *The Shoemaker's Holiday* (1599):

O the month of May, the merry month of May,
So frolick, so gay, and so green, so green, so green!
O, and then did I unto my true love say:
"Sweet Peg, thou shalt be my summer's queen!"

Now here is Ariel's famous song from *The Tempest* (1610):

Full fathom five thy father lies;
Of his bones are coral made;
Those are pearls that were his eyes:
Nothing of him that doth fade
But doth suffer a sea-change
Into something rich and strange.
Sea-nymphs hourly ring his knell:
Hark! now I hear them,—ding-dong, bell.

The difference here is one of kind, not of degree. Everything Shakespeare touches suffers that sea-change into something rich and strange. Except for Marlowe at his most Shakespearean and some of Ben Jonson, I had never read any of Shakespeare's competitors before that flight. Some of them are good, but he is as far from them as he is from us. Like mediocre sitcoms, they rely on caricatured personalities and bad foreign accents for laughs. If these are the genre's second tier, perhaps it isn't such a loss if the majority of Elizabethan and Jacobean drama is forgotten.

That doesn't mean these other dramas aren't fun to read. Several of the plays are set in the London of their day, so I was glad to be reading them on my way to that city, no matter how little it might now resemble its earlier self.

We spent just one night in London, at the Naval and Military Club, a private club off Leicester Square where the beds were cheaper than at any hotel in town. The place had a distinctly antiquarian air. Near the fireplace in the sitting room hung a large portrait of Prince Philip, the club's ex officio president. I wondered when he'd last paid a visit. Midtown Manhattan has many old gentlemen's clubs, forced by the end of "club life" to serve as glorified hotels. (In fact, it was a reciprocal agreement with one such place that allowed us in the door at the Naval and Military.) But there was something quintessentially British about this one. The name suggested the days of empire, when the British navy was a dominant force in the world. This in turn suggested the early years of the last century, the years when the Classics were being bought in the hundreds of thousands.

I finished the last of the Elizabethan plays—Philip Massinger's *A New Way to Pay Old Debts* (1625), also set in London—on our train ride to Cambridge, and then I gave up reading the Shelf for the rest of the trip. J.P. had studied at the university for a term while in college, and he'd remained in touch with the don, John Murrell, who had run his exchange program. We met John for lunch on our first day in town. At the end of the meal, he offered to take us on a tour the next morning.

John seemed to me the picture of the charming Cambridge don, wearing his learning and his deep sense of history with ease. He'd grown up in Rugby, where as he explained it the two requirements of a true gentleman were to know Virgil and play a good game of football. ("Of course, I mean *Rugby* football," he added—as opposed to Association football, or soccer, first played in its present form on a field in Cambridge.) John was also a committed amerophile who took great pleasure in showing his home to Yanks. His tour was well practiced but never forced.

Early on, we went to King's College, one of the oldest and largest of Cambridge's colleges. Its chapel, John explained, was begun in the middle of the fifteenth century by Henry VI. Like Gaudi's Sagrada Familia, it took more than a hundred years to complete. All of the building's stained glass—among the largest collections in the world—was taken down and placed in storage during the blitz, and for years afterward the windows of the chapel had remained boarded up.

All the buildings we passed had stories attached to them, some of these stories dating back just a generation or two, others as old as the town itself. Each time we passed one of the town's many Latin inscriptions, John would read it out loud to us and then preface his translation with, "Now, my Latin tells me that this means . . ."

* * *

During lunch, he asked if any of us knew why stars and stripes adorned the American flag.

"Well, the thirteen stripes are the original colonies, and the fifty stars are the states."

"Yes," he allowed. "But why stars and stripes? Why not chevrons, or fleurs-de-lis?"

After a bit of bumbling, we all had to admit that we didn't know. In fact, the question had never occurred to us. He took mischievous pleasure in stumping us on our own turf, and I was sure that we weren't the first to fail his test. When we'd finished our pints and pub food, he brought us to Saint Peter's Chapel, once the home of the first of Cambridge's colleges. On the wall near the altar was a small plaque commemorating Godfrey Washington, a onetime fellow of St. Peter's and cousin to General George Washington. Above the plaque was the Washington family crest, consisting of, yes, red and white stars and stripes.

Near the end of the tour, John brought us to Emmanuel College and showed us its portraits of famous alumni, which included John Harvard.

"When the first American college was founded in his name," John Murrell explained, "they modeled it after his old university."

I mentioned that Harvard had retained this British model until the late nineteenth century, when Charles Eliot, who was then its president, enacted a number of major reforms. John seemed almost impressed by this bit of trivia. Then he showed us a large bronze plaque, given by Harvard to Emmanuel College at the beginning of the twentieth century and now proudly displayed in a broom closet outside the chapel.

★ ★ ★

After the tour, we dropped John at his house and walked back through town. The streets of Cambridge are lined with many of the same stores you would find at an upscale mall in the United States, but the buildings that hold these stores are centuries old. My own college campus at Princeton has the same Gothic architecture that I saw everywhere in Cambridge, but ours is an ersatz version, mostly built in the late nineteenth century and the early twentieth century.

It was Sunday, and we were halfway back to Paul's flat when the church bells started ringing. Every college at the university has a chapel, and there are many other churches besides. In fact, the ratio of churches to churchgoers in the city must be steadily approaching one to one. The sound of these bells was overwhelming, but the people around us went about their business as if they heard nothing at all. I had no idea how many of them still went to church with any regularity, but they all took for granted that the bells would ring at this time each week.

Before leaving town, we went to see a performance of Handel's *Messiah* in one of those churches. The place was filled. The soloists were professional singers who had once studied voice at Cambridge. The chorus consisted of the choir from one of the colleges and a local children's choir. A group specializing in medieval and Renaissance instruments provided accompaniment.

As I listened and watched, I felt that I had arrived in a world where the past wasn't something one studied, but the place where one lived. I don't mean this in the pejorative sense of resisting change or being unwilling to meet the present reality. I just mean that every square foot of the town carried some historical association, an association that wasn't hidden by present use but was available to all. *Against this tree, Newton sat. In this building, Crick and Watson studied.* I'm sure most of the people listening to the concert didn't know the history that surrounded them in the same detail that John did; they couldn't have articulated it to a stranger in the way he had. But they didn't need to "know" it. It was simply there.

The day after our return to New York, I started reading Blaise Pascal. Over two months, I had managed to work myself ahead of schedule. For the first time in weeks, I felt no rush to get through the remaining volumes. This was fortunate, because Pascal demands time. He does so not because of length but by suggestion: his words expand to fit whatever space you allow them.

Pascal was born in the Auvergne region of France in 1623, in the middle of the Protestant Reformation. He was educated mostly in the sciences, and within his own lifetime he was known as a mathematician and physicist. But he was also a Jansenist, a member of a rigorous sect of post-Reformation Catholics that was ultimately declared heretical by the Vatican, and he is remembered now because of his religious writing, collected posthumously and published under the title *Pensées* (1670). These "thoughts" were the notes for his *Apology for the Christian Religion,* which he didn't live to complete. Because the book was left in outline form, it seems sketchy, even aphoristic. But certain parts are like kernels, deceptively small for all that they contain, waiting to burst open with the application of a little heat.

Today, Pascal is probably best known for his so-called "wager." "Reason can decide nothing here," he writes about the realm of religious belief. "There is an infinite chaos which separates us.

A game is being played at the extremity of this infinite distance where heads or tails will turn up. What will you wager?" Neither bet, for or against the existence of God, can be truly supported by reason, says Pascal. But still you must wager—"It is not optional." So which should we choose?

"Let us weigh the gain and the loss in wagering that God is. Let us estimate these two chances. If you gain, you gain all; if you lose, you lose nothing. Wager then without hesitation that He is."

It's sometimes assumed that Pascal, as a trained mathematician, attempted to inject rationalism into religion. But his rationalism is a very strange kind whose first principle is, "Reason can decide nothing here." Pascal is essentially pessimistic about reason as a tool for answering the most pressing questions. "Who has put me here?" he writes. "By whose order and direction have this place and time been alloted to me? The eternal silence of these infinite spaces frightens me." For Pascal, this fear demands religion. In turn, this demand brings religion into being. And the existence of religion calls out for its proof.

"Men despise religion," Pascal writes, "they hate it, and fear it is true. To remedy this, we must begin by showing that religion is not contrary to reason; that it is venerable, to inspire respect for it; then we must make it lovable, to make good men hope it is true; finally, we must prove it is true."

There is something cockeyed about this approach. Shouldn't the first step be to establish truth, since the "lovability" of religion is otherwise basically moot? It would seem that Pascal himself is among those who hate religion and fear that it's true. More precisely, he hates religion and *knows* that it's true. He can't live in a world where it isn't true, and he takes this fact as a proof in itself. This is why the more pressing task is making religion "lovable." In Pascal's world, the ringing of the church bells on every corner is constant and unavoidable; it continues until the sound threatens to drive him mad.

If I seem unsympathetic to Pascal, quite the opposite is true. I find him exactly right about our fragility in the world. The eternal silence of these infinite spaces frightens me, too. And there is a beauty to many of the things with which Pascal has chosen to fill that space. "Man is but a reed," he writes, "the most feeble thing in nature, but he is a thinking reed."

One day in the week before Christmas, Jim, his fiancée Alyson, and I took a walk we had taken many times earlier in the year, uptown on York Avenue from my parents' apartment to the complex of hospitals in the upper sixties. We were going, not to Memorial, where Mimi had spent many of her last days, but across the street to New York Hospital, where, late the previous night, my sister had given birth to the newest member of our family.

At the hospital, I sat in a chair beside Alice's bed and held the newborn Leo in the crook of my arm. He stretched about the length from my palm to my elbow. He didn't cry; he only lay there quietly. He seemed to be awake, but he could hardly open his eyes.

It had been a difficult year in many ways—surely the most difficult of my own life. We had lost someone we all loved very much. Illness had reminded me once again of my own feebleness. But here I was being given a moment of simple joy. This fragile creature in my arms was beautiful, and his fragility was part of what made him so.

During the week between Christmas and the New Year, I went skiing with my family. I was still recovering from my surgery and from Lyme disease, so I couldn't take more than a few runs each day. I mostly sat at home, finishing up the Shelf. By then, I was through with the Classics proper. Only the two supplemental volumes remained. The first supplement was the introductory volume, with its index and "Reader's Guide," placed at the end of the set because the earliest volumes had been prepared before Eliot and Neilson had any clear sense of the overall shape of their collection. Last, there was a volume of Lectures on the Harvard Classics, which was added to the Shelf about a year after publication. These volumes fulfilled Eliot's goal of making the Classics a practical course of study for the uninitiated reader.

It was anticlimactic to close out my reading with these volumes, but I was glad to have come to them when I did. Part of the charm of the Harvard Classics had been their mystery and my confusion, not knowing from week to week what would come next and how it might relate to what had already passed. If there had been some grand plan all along (and I knew now that there had not), I would have been happy enough not to know it. As it was, the lectures offered an excuse to end the year with some retrospection. I had now been given a map to this strange city I'd been visiting. Although this map might serve as a guide in the future, I was glad that I'd had a chance to wander around without it.

And before I got to the lectures, there was Eliot's introduction, the ten-page document that I'd read so many times at my
grandmother's house, the words that had made me want to read
the Classics in the first place. The satisfaction of checking titles
off of a list had become much less important to me as the year
went on. Admittedly, though, I felt a thrill at reading these few
familiar pages now that I had finished all the volumes that came
before them. It was natural to wonder what, if anything, I had
managed to achieve.

"Within the limits of fifty volumes, containing about 22,000
pages," Eliot writes, "I was to provide the means of obtaining
such a knowledge of ancient and modern literature as seems
essential to the twentieth-century idea of a cultivated man."
What exactly was this twentieth-century idea of a cultivated man
to which Eliot refers? Now that I had read those 22,000 pages,
did I have any better idea?

Eliot makes an effort to answer the question himself. "The
best acquisition of a cultivated man is a liberal frame of mind
or way of thinking," he writes, "but there must be added to that
possession acquaintance with the prodigious store of recorded
discoveries, experiences, and reflections which humanity in its
intermittent and irregular progress from barbarism to civilization has acquired and laid up." Over the course of reading the
Shelf, I had come to a much greater understanding of Eliot's idea
of culture as internal improvement, rather than as a set of char-
acteristics or a collection of knowledge. From Plato to Emerson,
the best authors in the Classics embody a particular approach
to learning, rather than merely conveying a set of facts. Para-
doxically, one of the great lessons of Eliot's "prodigious store
of recorded discoveries, experiences, and reflections" is that one
must always struggle to see things with fresh eyes. As Emerson

says, we should be sure to read the books of Cicero, Locke, and Bacon, but we should also remember that "Cicero, Locke and Bacon were only young men in libraries when they wrote these books."

And yet this caution must be balanced with an appreciation for how much the best of the past has to offer us. If it is true that the goal is intellectual self-sufficiency, it's also true that we need the wisdom of those who came before, if only to teach us how eventually to do without it. We need those young men in their libraries to remind us that we might achieve just as much as they did.

To strike this balance we need to have both the confidence and the discernment to take from the Classics the things we can use and to set aside the rest. I was hardly done with some of these books when I knew that I would never return to them, whereas others will probably remain touchstones throughout my life. But again, it was the books themselves that taught me this. Before I read these two superficially similar books, I couldn't have known that Thomas à Kempis's *The Imitation of Christ* would mean little to me while Pascal's *Pensées* would mean so much. Many of my favorite works in the Classics, such as Dana's *Two Years before the Mast* or Haskell's letter from Gettysburg, had been entirely unfamiliar to me when I started. While reading these books, I needed to judge their worth for myself. But first I needed that outdated body—the clerisy, the intellectual elite—to tell me which books to read.

This clerisy, already a dying breed when the Classics were compiled, is shown at its best and its worst in these last volumes. The reader's guide is wonderfully flexible, open to the many different goals one might have in mind when approaching the Shelf. It suggests dozens of different paths through the Classics—by subject matter, genre, or historical progression. Just about the only method the guide *doesn't* suggest is the one that I used, reading the Shelf from start to finish. After this guide comes an index that fills several hundred pages. I had never paid attention to this part of the volume before—understandably, I suppose, because indexes don't make exciting reading. But the exhaustiveness of the index reminded me that the Classics were meant to be a real resource for readers, rather than a set of objects taking up space on a shelf. And I imagine that I will make use of the index in the future when I want to find some idea or quotation I vaguely remember.

The volume of lectures had a mixed effect on me. It gave me a fuller picture of the time and place—New England academe in the first decade of the twentieth century—that had produced the Classics. The lectures also serve as an introduction to the men who assisted Eliot and Neilson in choosing the books, and it was fascinating to read about the attitudes that informed those choices. For example, Eliot wrote that he had excluded nineteenth-century fiction only because it was readily available to the common reader, and I knew that Collier had resisted including novels for this reason. But in a lecture on biography, a man named William Roscoe Thayer offers a different justification for the omission. "In no art has the process of vulgarization gone so far as in fiction," he writes. "The novelist to-day dares not paint goodness or greatness; his upper limit is mediocrity; his lower is depravity, and he tends more and more to exploit the lower." The Classics emerged at the beginning of the short era when the novel was the supreme narrative genre, and it's amusing to see the form so ill-treated. But this passage was also a personal reminder that we dismiss

the most popular art forms—in our own era, movies and
television—at our peril.

Other lectures made me eager to go back to my favorite volumes. The very best of them rise to the level of literature themselves. Given my recent encounter with Wordsworth, I was
naturally eager to read the lectures on poetry. "A poem is a frag-
ment of life rounded into momentary completeness," writes
Carleton Noyes, a professor of poetry at Harvard, in his introduction to the genre. "It compels the chaos of immediate sense
impressions into forms of beauty, and so it builds a fairer
world." Elsewhere, Noyes adds that "the poet is not final; nor
is poetry, with the appreciator, an end in itself. In the result it
sends us back to life, to possess the world more abundantly in
ourselves."

With that, I was done. I can't say I felt any great sense of relief
or accomplishment on closing the last volume. But I did wonder how many people had ever made their way through the
Shelf as I had. "My purpose in selecting the Harvard Classics,"
Eliot writes in his introduction, "was to provide the literary
materials from which a careful and persistent reader might gain
a fair view of the progress of man observing, recording, inventing, and imagining from the earliest historical times to the
close of the nineteenth century." I wanted to believe that Eliot's
fifteen-minutes-a-day readers had really existed, that some of
them had come home from work one evening in late 1909 or
early 1910 and read the first five pages of the *Autobiography* of
Benjamin Franklin. Perhaps sometime in 1917 or 1919, a few
of those few closed this book of lectures, feeling that, through

pleasurable dedication, they had reached a certain level of cultivation. And it would never have occurred to those men and
women to put this word, "cultivation," in quotation marks. It
meant that something important, something alive, had been
buried inside them, planted for them to nurture. It meant also
that they themselves had been planted in something, that they
had been taken out of their own time and place and made a
part of something universally human. They shut the book,
they went to sleep, and in the morning they woke at the same
time as always and went to work. And they worked—as feeble
as reeds. But thinking reeds.

I believe a few such careful and persistent readers are still out
there. Perhaps the Harvard Classics are no longer the best way
for them to achieve cultivation. It's easy to find ways in which
the Shelf might be updated or improved. After gaining from the
lectures an inside look into the contingencies that gave rise to
the Classics as we know them, it's tempting to ask: how would
I do it?

I suppose there are things I would change about the set if I
could. The most obvious step would be to expand them to include more non-Western works, more works by women, more
modern works. But even if we put those issues aside, if we take
the Harvard Classics to be essentially Eurocentric and patriar-
chal, there are a number of decisions that a different cohort of
Eurocentric patriarchs would have made differently than Eliot
and his colleagues. Why not the *Iliad* instead of the *Odyssey*? Why
so much Robert Burns and no Aristotle? For God's sake, why
John Woolman?

But then I think, on reflection, that I wouldn't change a thing.
Now that I've read all 22,000 pages of the Classics—the whole

five feet of the Five-Foot Shelf—I wouldn't wish away its eccentricities, its particular emphases and lacunae. Of course it's an incomplete picture, but it isn't final; it isn't an end in itself. I can only hope that it sends me back to life, to possess the world more abundantly in myself.

Afterword, or "I Shall Go On in the Same Way"

The Harvard Classics Shelf of Fiction

Benvenuto Cellini was born in Florence in 1500. He began to write his life's story in 1558. In between, he became the most distinguished goldsmith in Renaissance Italy, as well as a leading sculptor; he flourished in an artistic circle that included Michelangelo; he fought in the sack of Rome; and he witnessed the arrival of the plague in Italy. Over the course of his career, he fell into and out of favor with many popes and one king of France, and he was a rival to several cardinals. He committed at least two murders—one to avenge the murder of his younger brother—and was generally quick to solve disputes with his dagger. He was brought up on charges of using one of his young female models "after the Italian fashion" (the implication, left untranslated here, being that he was a *soddomitaccio*). Another model bore him a daughter, whom he never saw after the first days of her life. Along the way, he was exiled from virtually every city where he spent any amount of time.

As a precursor to the modern memoir, Cellini's *Autobiography* (1558) ranks beside the Confessions of Augustine and Rousseau. But Cellini writes without apology. His book is no confession; it's a justification. He admits as much from the start. "All men of whatsoever quality they be, who have done anything of excellence," he says, "or which may properly resemble excellence, ought, if they are persons of truth and honesty, to describe their life with their own hand." This, then, is his goal: to display his excellence to the world.

A great deal in Cellini's *Autobiography* almost certainly never happened (this is another way in which he blazed a trail for today's memoirist), but the reader forgives almost anything under the sheer force of his personality. Anyone who wants to write about his own life will find in Cellini's outsized narrative a stirring example. Yet as I read now through my own pages, I find that Cellini isn't even mentioned in my chapter on September, the month when I read his *Autobiography*. And I realize that I haven't written the book I set out to write.

In some ways, I suppose no one ever writes the book he sets out to write. The process of writing is a series of compromises by which the ideal gives way to the actual. But I mean something more prosaic than that: the book I intended to write was essentially a comedy, about a feckless, somewhat lost young man who shuts himself away from the modern world and its cultural white noise—from life as it's lived in his own time and place—in order to immerse himself in classic literature. By the end of this story, I thought, the young man might learn a few easy lessons, and we could all share some laughs along the way. But writing that book proved impossible; the story line didn't cooperate.

The story of the past year for me was not the story of reading books, but the story of a loss that couldn't be assimilated into a comedy. It was also the story of an illness that, although it passed, brought me back to a time when my life was in real danger. It was the story of witnessing the birth of one child and the growth of several others. Last, it was the story of reading these books. But even that story didn't turn out the way I expected it to. There were no simple lessons or pat answers. Nor was there any comical shutting out of the world—the one common feature of all these books was precisely the fact that they kept sending me back *into* the world.

Although I didn't write the comedy I set out to write, at least I can end my book in the way so many good comedies end: with a wedding. In the first week of January, my cousin Michael and his fiancée Emily were married at the Church of Saint Ignatius Loyola, where we had said good-bye to Michael's mother eight months earlier. The same priest, Father Katsouris, officiated. Paul flew back from Cambridge to act as best man. Jim and I were among the groomsmen. Alice and Len's two daughters were the flower girls. My parents and my aunt Jaime served as stand-ins for the parents of the groom. And in the second pew, my two-week-old nephew Leo slept.

During the reception, I danced on my surgically repaired knee. And after it was all done, I went home to read *Tom Jones*.

Despite the controversy surrounding its initial publication, the Harvard Classics proved wildly popular, and Collier was eager to duplicate this success. Though they had resisted Eliot's effort to include several English novels in the original Shelf, the publishers now proposed a second set, dedicated entirely to the novel and a few representative works of shorter fiction. Eliot agreed to edit the Harvard Classics Shelf of Fiction. As in the initial effort, most of the work of selecting and introducing the volumes was delegated to William Neilson. In addition to short biographical notes similar to those included in the Classics, Neilson wrote a number of essays describing the history of the novel in several national traditions—English, American, French, German, Russian, and Scandinavian.

I was about halfway through the Classics when I found a full set of the Fiction Shelf on eBay and decided that I would read it next. This plan wasn't as ambitious as reading the Five-Foot Shelf. The Fiction Shelf is much shorter—just twenty volumes. Because several of the novels span multiple volumes, the total number of works is actually less than twenty. I first came to love literature through the novel; it remains the form I love best.

As I write these words, I'm most of the way through the Fiction Shelf. It's an odd vantage point from which to look back on my year with the Harvard Classics. The works I've been reading were kept off the Five-Foot Shelf because Collier worried that too many potential subscribers would already own them. That is, they were kept out because they were too popular. Although works by some of the authors here—Jane Austen, Charles Dickens—still have popular appeal, most are read only by students and specialists. It's been suggested that the day of the novel as a truly popular literary form is ending. If so, it had a fairly short career.

There are many different ways to define the novel, and each definition suggests a different life span for the genre. Throughout most of literary history, verse has been the preferred form for fictional narratives, but there is at least one surviving example of the long prose fiction—Lucius Apuleius's *The Golden Ass*— from the early Roman empire. Then there is *The Tale of Genji*, written by a Japanese noblewoman in the eleventh century. And any contemporary reader of the novel would recognize *Don Quixote* or Rabelais's sixteenth-century *Gargantua and Pantagruel* as meeting the descriptions of the form.

The various experiments with the form over the past century have encouraged the most inclusive definitions. But for the average reader (or the average scholar, for that matter) at the turn of the twentieth century, the term "novel" referred to the realist novel perfected in the nineteenth century, a genre that is actually quite young. Of the many works of prose fiction included in the original Five-Foot Shelf, only Manzoni's *The Betrothed*, published in 1826, qualified in Charles Eliot's eyes as a novel. In a general introduction to the fiction series, he writes that *Don Quixote* has "a character quite distinct from that of the nineteenth century novel," but he doesn't explain what the difference actually is. In another introduction, Neilson states unequivocally that "the novel first emerged as a definite literary type in the eighteenth century." Henry Fielding's *The History of Tom Jones, a Foundling*, published in 1749, is the first book included in the set.

Leaving aside the claims of *The Golden Ass* or *The Tale of Genji*, it seems particularly fitting to begin with *Tom Jones*, because Fielding himself felt quite certain that he was initiating a new form. One mark of this new form—which Fielding labeled a "history," not a "novel"—was to be its structural flexibility. "My reader then is not to be surprized," Fielding writes in one of his book's many chapters of commentary, "if, in the course of this work, he shall find some chapters very short, and others altogether as long; some that contain only the time of a single day, and others that comprise years; in a word, if my history sometimes seems to stand still, and sometimes to fly. For all which I shall not look on myself as accountable to any court of critical jurisdiction whatever: for as I am, in reality, the founder of a new province of writing, so I am at liberty to make what laws I please therein."

Daniel Defoe and Samuel Richardson had already proved the popularity of long prose narratives in eighteenth-century

England, but Fielding considered their work sentimental and unrealistic, and he meant to correct them by showing man as he actually is. "The provision, then, which we have here made," Fielding warned his readers, "is no other than *Human Nature*." It was for this reason—to capture all of life's messiness—that he insisted on complete structural freedom. For many subsequent critics, this effort at verisimilitude became the defining characteristic of the novel. As practiced by Fielding, it meant the freedom to include lots of drinking, swearing, and sex.

The novel begins on the estate—one of the largest in the county—of Squire Allworthy. The descriptive name has the air of allegory but, though the squire is indeed the worthiest figure in the novel, even he is not idealized by Fielding. Allworthy is a childless widower when he returns from a trip to London to find an abandoned infant in his bed. This foundling is assumed to be the son of a poor local girl named Jenny Jones, and he is given her family name, although Allworthy raises him as his own son.

When Tom Jones is still an infant, the squire's sister marries a man named Blifil and gives birth to a son of her own, and the two boys are raised and educated together. Tom is wild and mischievous but ultimately lovable; the young Blifil displays all the external manifestations of a saint while remaining coldly self-interested on the inside. Their relationship mirrors the relationship of Fielding's bawdy but humane novel to its more "correct," but less alive, competitors. It also raises questions about outward appearance and inner reality that would continue to occupy the novel throughout the form's history.

Jones and Blifil come eventually to compete for the love of a girl named Sophia. ("Compete" may be the wrong word; Blifil's main interest is to keep Tom from what he wants.) Tom and Sophia's courtship is complicated considerably by Tom's tendency to get drunk and wind up in bed with other girls. It's also complicated by a number of other authorial obstacles, and we are left to wonder if the two lovers will ever find each other again. But the book ends—as I said, the conventions of the form demand it—with a marriage.

In truth, *Tom Jones* suffers from its structural bagginess, from chapters that are too long or too short. Over time, the novel would become more disciplined, eventually reaching a level of precision comparable to that found in the best verse. Just half a century after Fielding, Jane Austen wrote what may still be the most expertly composed novels in the English language; and her *Pride and Prejudice* follows *Tom Jones* in the Fiction Shelf. Like Fielding, Austen writes comedies, and like Fielding she ends them with marriages. But she's much more controlled in her work. No scene is presented that doesn't have some bearing on her story. If one scene suffices to give a fair sense of a character, she won't give us two. If one line suffices, she won't give us a scene.

The result is more satisfying in almost every way, but it also comes with a cost. Historically, most novelists have accepted Fielding's idea that the novel represents an unprecedented effort to document "human nature," to convey life as it's actually lived. They've also grappled with the risk inherent in correcting Fielding's excesses: the novel becomes less lifelike as it becomes more formally exact.

But one thing the past year has reminded me is that books aren't life. If it's satisfying to find shape and control on the page, that may be precisely because they often seem absent from the world. Books draw meaning from life, but they also give meaning in return. For this reason, the difference between books and life—and, by extension, between appearance and reality—has been one of the novel's important subjects dating back as far as *Don Quixote*, which is ultimately the story of man who goes out to test life against what he has found in books. There, the difference is used as a source of comedy, but it's just as often put to tragic ends, as it is in *Anna Karenina*.

Tolstoy's novel is one of the last works in the Fiction Shelf, and to my mind it's the greatest novel ever written. The title character, Anna, is "the wife of one of the most important personages in Petersburg, and . . . a Petersburg *grande dame*." But she falls for an army officer, Vronsky. She does so in part because romantic novels have suggested to her that another kind of life is possible. (Similar reading prompts Emma Bovary's affair in that other high point of nineteenth-century realism, *Madame Bovary*.) Eventually, this choice leads to Anna's death. But the book doesn't end there.

Throughout the novel, there has been a second and parallel story line. It concerns Konstantin Levin and his wife Kitty, whose relationship serves throughout the book as a counterpoint to Anna and Vronsky's. Early in the novel, Kitty turns down a proposal from Levin because she is expecting one from Vronsky, but after Anna and Vronsky take up together, Kitty accepts a second proposal from Levin.

From the book's beginning, Levin has struggled to come to terms with the meaning of goodness, and particularly with what it means to be genuine rather than false. He's a rich landowner, but he spends time working in the fields with his serfs. This work provides fleeting feelings of authenticity. Many readers find these so-called "threshing scenes" rather boring, a distraction from the romantic tragedy at the heart of the novel. But I am moved by them.

After Anna's death, Tolstoy dedicates the last hundred pages to Levin and Kitty. In the book's last chapter, Levin leans out a window to look up at the sky during a storm. "Well, what is it perplexes me?" he asks himself. "What am I about? To me individually, to my heart has been revealed a knowledge beyond all doubt, and unattainable by reason, and here I am obstinately trying to express that knowledge in reason and words."

This is the struggle of literature: to express the knowledge of the heart in reason and words, even if that expression will always fall short. As he engages in this struggle, Levin considers the stars. Intellectually, he knows that they're fixed in place, whereas the earth moves around the sun. But from where he's standing, the stars do, in fact, move, while his own position remains fixed:

> And could the astronomers have understood and calculated anything, if they had taken into account all the complicated and varied motions of the earth? All the marvellous conclusions they have reached about the distances, weights, movements, and deflections of the heavenly bodies are only founded on the apparent motions of the heavenly bodies about a stationary earth, on that very motion I see before me now, which has been so for millions of men during long ages, and was and will be always alike, and can always be trusted. And just as the conclusions of the astronomers would have been vain and uncertain if not founded on observations of the seen heavens, in relation to a single meridian and a single horizon, so would my conclusions be vain and uncertain if not founded on that conception of right, which has been and will be always alike for all men.

Levin's thoughts are interrupted by Kitty's arrival. She asks if he is worrying about anything, and she looks at his face. "But she could not have seen in his face," Tolstoy adds, "if a flash of lightning had not hidden the stars and revealed it. In that flash she saw his face distinctly, and seeing him calm and happy, she smiled at him." Levin is preparing to tell Kitty about the breakthrough he's made when she asks him to check on a room the servants have prepared for a visitor. He decides then that he won't tell her: "It is a secret for me alone, of vital importance for me, and not to be put into words."

This new feeling has not changed me, has not made me happy and enlightened all of a sudden, as I had dreamed, just like the feeling for my child. There was no surprise in this either. Faith— or not faith—I don't know what it is—but this feeling has come just as imperceptibly through suffering, and has taken firm root in my soul.

I shall go on in the same way, losing my temper with Ivan the coachman, falling into angry discussions, expressing my opinions tactlessly; there will be still the same wall between the holy of holies of my soul and other people, even my wife; I shall still go on scolding her for my own terror, and being remorseful for it; I shall still be as unable to understand with my reason why I pray, and I shall still go on praying; but my life now, my whole life apart from anything that can happen to me, every minute of it is no more meaningless, as it was before, but it has the positive meaning of goodness, which I have the power to put into it.

In many ways, this is how I feel about having finished the Classics: I shall go on in the same way. Nothing in my life is going to

change in any visible fashion. But these books have helped me
to find meaning in events—illness and loss as well as moments
of great joy—that didn't make any sense to me. At the same
time, life helped me make sense of these books. And so it will
continue to go, for although I have read through the whole five
feet, I'll never be finished with them.

Acknowledgments

Anyone who has read this far will have some sense of how much I have depended on the generosity and support of my family, particularly my parents, James and Nancy Beha. I offer thanks first and foremost to them, to Jim and Alyson Beha, and to Mary Alice and Len Teti. Thanks to Sanny Beha for prayers and newspaper clippings, and to all the members of the Escott, Gans, Radloff, and Teti families.

I owe a great debt to my friends, particularly to three who read early drafts: Alexis Rudisill, Bret Asbury, and Brian DeLeeuw.

This book was born when I mentioned my desire to read the Classics and write about them to Sally Wofford-Girand. Her enthusiasm for the project was immediate and proved sustaining. Thanks to her and to Melissa Sarver at Brick House.

I'm very lucky to have found a home for this book at Grove. Thanks to Morgan Entrekin for signing it on. Thanks to Martin Wilson, Deb Seager, and Charles Rue Woods. Above all, thanks to Jofie Ferrari-Adler, who has been, from day one, the ideal editor but has become, since then, a great friend.

Thanks to the Harvard University Archives for access to the Charles W. Eliot Papers and permission to use images from the papers, including the advertisement at the front of this book. Thanks to Ann and Rob Radloff for putting me up in Boston.

In addition to the volumes of the Shelf itself, I consulted a number of valuable books while writing *The Whole Five Feet,* including Henry James's *Charles W. Eliot,* Joan Shelley Rubin's *The Making of Middlebrow Culture,* and Lawrence Levine's *Highbrow/Lowbrow.*

Lastly, the Harvard Classics are available, for free and in their entirety, at Bartleby.com, an invaluable site of which I made much use while writing this book.

Appendix I

The Five-Foot Shelf

Volume I	*His Autobiography,* by Benjamin Franklin
	Journal, by John Woolman
	Fruits of Solitude, by William Penn
Volume II	*The Apology, Phaedo,* and *Crito* of Plato
	The Golden Sayings of Epictetus
	The Meditations of Marcus Aurelius
Volume III	*Essays, Civil and Moral* and *The New Atlantis,* by Francis Bacon
	Areopagitica and *Tractate on Education,* by John Milton
	Religio Medici, by Sir Thomas Browne
Volume IV	*Complete Poems Written in English,* by John Milton
Volume V	*Essays* and *English Traits,* by Ralph Waldo Emerson
Volume VI	*Poems and Songs,* by Robert Burns
Volume VII	*The Confessions* of Saint Augustine
	The Imitation of Christ, by Thomas à Kempis
Volume VIII	*Agamemnon, The Libation-Bearers, The Furies,* and *Prometheus Bound* of Aeschylus
	Oedipus the King and *Antigone* of Sophocles
	Hippolytus and *The Bacchae* of Euripides
	The Frogs of Aristophanes

Volume XXIV   *On Taste, On the Sublime and Beautiful,*
                  Reflections on the French Revolution, and
                  A Letter to a Noble Lord, by Edmund Burke
Volume XXV   *Autobiography* and *On Liberty,*
                  by John Stuart Mill
                  Characteristics, Inaugural Address
                  at Edinburgh, and *Sir Walter Scott,*
                  by Thomas Carlyle
Volume XXVI   *Life Is a Dream,* by Pedro Calderón de la Barca
                  Polyeucte, by Pierre Corneille
                  Phaedra, by Jean Racine
                  Tartuffe, by Molière
                  Minna von Barnhelm,
                  by Gotthold Ephraim Lessing
                  Wilhelm Tell, by Friedrich von Schiller
Volume XXVII   English Essays: Sidney to Macaulay
Volume XXVIII   Essays: English and American
Volume XXIX   *The Voyage of the Beagle,* by Charles Darwin
Volume XXX   Scientific Papers
Volume XXXI   *The Autobiography* of Benvenuto Cellini
Volume XXXII   Literary and Philosophical Essays
Volume XXXIII   Voyages and Travels: Ancient and Modern
Volume XXXIV   *Discourse on Method,* by René Descartes
                  Letters on the English, by Voltaire
                  On Inequality among Mankind and
                  Profession of Faith of a Savoyard Vicar,
                  by Jean-Jacques Rousseau
                  Of Man, Being the First Part of Leviathan,
                  by Thomas Hobbes
Volume XXXV   *The Chronicles* of Jean Froissart
                  The Holy Grail, by Sir Thomas Malory
                  A Description of Elizabethan England,
                  by William Harrison

Appendix II

The Harvard Classics Shelf of Fiction

THE WHOLE FIVE FEET

Christopher R. Beha

ABOUT THIS GUIDE

We hope that this interview and essay
will enhance your reading experience
of Christopher R. Beha's *The Whole Five Feet*. They are
meant to enrich your enjoyment of the book.

More reading group guides and additional information,
including summaries, author tours, and author sites for
other fine Grove Press titles, may be found on
our Web site, www.groveatlantic.com.

A conversation with Christopher R. Beha
about *The Whole Five Feet*

Now that a bit of time has passed, are there things about your year with the Five Foot Shelf that you wish you'd done differently?

I'm tempted to say that I wish I'd taken more time with the volumes. You could spend a lifetime on some of these books. In fact, many scholars have. But the truth is that without the rigid, albeit completely artificial, timeline I put myself on, I would never have read most of these books. Now that I have read them all, I can go back and take my time over those I loved best.

And which volume did you "love best"? You have to pick just one.

The cop out answer—that I can't pick just one—happens to be true in this case. But if I must, I'll choose Emerson's essays, which I already knew quite well before encountering them in the Harvard Classics and which have long been favorites of mine. I'd probably give another answer on another day, though. I also have particular affections for those books, like Cellini's *Autobiography* and Dana's *Two Years Before the Mast*, that I would never have read had I not found them in the Five Foot Shelf.

Which was your least favorite?

Simply as a reading experience, my least favorite was Darwin's *On the Origin of Species*. The historical and intellectual importance of Darwin's work can't be overstated. If anything, I suppose that some segments of the population are too quick to dismiss it, because they are unwillingly to grapple with its implications. But to the extent that a "classic" is a book that can be read and enjoyed by the "common reader," rather than just paid lip service, I'm not sure *Origin of Species* qualifies. Scientific writing creates a tricky question for canon-makers for two reasons: it's usually written for a specialized audience, and it isn't really meant to be permanent. That is, even the most far-sighted scientists expect their work to be altered and improved by new technology and later thinkers. This is where compiling a "great books" list differs as an exercise from using books to teach intellectual history.

What works do you think are missing from the Classics that you would include if you were putting out your own set?

Let's set aside the hundred years of literature that has been created since Charles Eliot compiled the Classics. Among works that Eliot might have chosen, the greatest lack is nineteenth-century writers like Nietzsche, Marx, and to some extent Freud—though much of his work was done after the Classics were compiled—whose writing had such a profound effect on the twentieth century. So I'd probably throw in Marx's *Capital* and a representative work of Nietzsche's, maybe *Thus Spoke Zarathustra*.

Have you heard a lot of stories from readers about their own (or their families') experiences with the Harvard Classics?

A number of people have told me that they own untouched sets of the Classics and that reading my book has inspired them at least to crack a few volumes. This has been nice. One person mentioned that I had "inspired" him to place his set on eBay, which I suppose means it's more likely to find its way to someone who will read it. . . .

Have the experiences you describe in the book changed you personally?

As readers of the book will know, this reading project was just one small part of a very turbulent year for me and my family. I lost someone I loved very much, but I also gained a new family member when my sister had a child. Of course, I didn't know any of this was in my future when I decided to read the Classics. I don't know how I would have met the challenges this year brought without these books. I also know that without these challenges much of the books' depths would have been lost on me. Life brings difficulties, but it also offers you something to meet those difficulties: the wisdom of those who came before and suffered these difficulties themselves. I think this understanding itself was the great lesson of the year for me, and it's changed the way I've read since then.

How did you know how much of yourself to put in The Whole Five Feet *and how much of the books?*

This was a tough problem, though it was made easier by the natural integration I mention above. Talking about the books meant talking about my life; talking about my life meant talking about the books. My editor also helped a lot. It's a common complaint about the contemporary publishing world that editors are too swamped with the business of publishing to do any real editing, but this wasn't my experience at all. My editor was a kind of collaborator in a way that was extremely valuable to me.

Since the completion of The Whole Five Feet, *have you reflected back on your time with the Harvard Classics—and, if so, what of the collection has stuck with you the most?*

I've been rereading some of the volumes, particularly the volumes of poetry. I'm more interested in what they have to say to me now, not in remembering what they said to me during my reading year. Just this morning I returned to Wordsworth's "Tintern Abbey," which is fitting in this context, because it is in part about the extent to which you can or can't revisit earlier selves, return mentally or physically to a past experience for nourishment:

That time is past,
And all its aching joys are now no more,
And all its dizzy raptures. Not for this
Faint I, nor mourn nor murmur, other gifts
Have followed; for such loss, I would believe,
Abundant recompence.

Having read all of the Harvard Classics, do you believe the set achieves the aims it was created to achieve?

The Shelf is idiosyncratic in many ways. To the extent that part of its purpose was canon-shaping, I think it was probably flawed to begin with, and it's certainly outdated now. (I'm setting aside entirely the question of whether such a purpose is even worthwhile; I happen to think it is, but that's a fight for another day.) To the extent that its purpose was to collect together a kind of curriculum and make it widely available, it certainly succeeded. And of course, it was a commercial venture—for the publishers, at least, if not for Eliot—and it succeeded incredibly as that. Several people have written to me to say that after reading my book they tracked down a set of the Classics. I found this extremely gratifying. There may now be better ways to receive an all-in-one-place experience of the "great books," but there aren't many, and if my book sends others to the Five Foot Shelf, I'm thrilled.

The Whole Five Feet takes place during a time of transition in your life. You had left a job, moved home with your parents. Your decision to read the Classics seemed in part a response to this feeling of being unsettled. How do things stand now?

After I finished *The Whole Five Feet* (but before it was published) I was hired as an editor at *Harper's* magazine, which is really a dream job for me. This in turn allowed me to move back out on my own.

So I'd say that everything is more settled now. I mention in the book that my real ambition was always to write fiction, and I'm back to doing that. I think my writing has been changed quite a bit, been nourished, by what I learned from the Classics. With all humility, it has made me want to write books that speak to people in the way that these books spoke to me.

Every Reader Finds Himself
Some Notes on the Book I Didn't Write
By Christopher R. Beha

1

A hundred years ago this month*, a man named Charles Eliot retired after forty years as president of Harvard, ending probably the most significant career in the history of American higher education. In some ways, Eliot's success was unlikely, though his story certainly began with promise enough. He was born into two of New England's old families—the Lymans on his mother's side, the Eliots on his father's—and he graduated third in his Harvard class in 1853. He was immediately hired as a tutor there, making him one of only thirteen faculty members at the college. Within a few years, he was elevated to an assistant professorship in chemistry and math.

So far, so good. But when his term came up, Eliot was passed over for a full professorship in favor of Wolcott Gibbs, a scientist with no previous connection to the college. This snub may have been justified: for all his later success as an administrator, Eliot never distinguished himself as a scholar, while Gibbs proved to be one of the great chemists of the age. But Gibbs's chief advantage at the time was that he wasn't Harvard-educated: while Eliot had received lots of drilling in Latin and Greek, Gibbs had studied chemistry in France and Germany, where he worked in the laboratory and gained practical research experience.

Eliot was invited to stay on at the college in a lesser capacity, but he opted instead to leave for Europe, where he spent the next

* This essay originally appeared in the May 2009 issue of *The Believer*.

two years studying the education systems that had given Gibbs such an advantage over him. In Germany and France he saw the research institutions whose specialization allowed for more sophisticated instruction than could be found anywhere in the States. The trip confirmed Eliot's belief that most of what passed for undergraduate education in America was a total waste of time. Upon his return he published his ideas about education reform in a series of well-regarded essays. These essays so impressed Harvard's board that they offered Eliot the college's presidency, just a few years after denying him a professorship. He was thirty-five. He would be seventy-five before he retired.

2

Astonishing changes occurred at Harvard over the course of Eliot's four-decade tenure. In 1869, the college had a faculty of 45, an undergraduate enrollment of 529 students, and an endowment of roughly two million dollars. An entering freshman took a fixed course of Latin, Greek, Mathematics, French, Elocution, and Ethics. Upperclassmen were allowed to choose from a handful of electives, but most of the curriculum was comprised of requirements for all four years. By 1909, Harvard had 194 faculty members, 2,238 undergraduates, and an endowment over twenty million. More significantly, students were given nearly total freedom in selecting their course of study, allowing for specialization and dramatically raising the level of upper-class course work. Eliot also oversaw the creation of the graduate program and profound changes in the already existing professional schools. (When he attempted to apply the innovation of written exams to Harvard's medical school, he was told that most of its students were illiterate.)

Freedom of study had been Eliot's greatest priority as an educational reformer, and it proved to be his lasting achievement. No longer did all students leave Harvard knowing Homer's Greek and

Cicero's Latin, but they knew the few subjects they had studied far better than they would have a half-century earlier. In particular, the new model allowed for advanced work in the natural sciences— the kind of work that had not been available to Eliot—which in turn became the foundation for serious graduate study, on the level of what could be found in Germany and France. Along with Johns Hopkins University (whose first president, Daniel Gilman, was one of Eliot's few peers in influence), Harvard awarded some of the earliest PhDs earned in America. Today, many scholars of American education date the birth of the modern American research university to the beginning of Eliot's tenure. Since then, Eliot's reforms have been reformed in turn, but by and large our college curricula look the way they look because of him.

3

If you have heard of Charles Eliot, it may be in connection with a project only tangentially related to his educational reforms. Throughout his career, Eliot was known to say that the necessary materials for a "liberal education" could fit on a five-foot shelf. As he neared retirement, he was approached by the publishers Collier and Son, who invited him to compile such a shelf. The resulting Harvard Classics—fifty-one-volumes that stretch from Homer to Darwin, stopping along the way for Plato and Shakespeare and Adam Smith—first appeared a century ago, in the same month as Eliot's retirement. "Dr. Eliot's Five Foot Shelf," as it was colloquially known, was the first of several "great books" sets released throughout the twentieth century. It was also a huge success, a major publishing phenomenon. Hundreds of thousands of these sets—millions of individual books—decorate home libraries to this day.

One of them still sits on shelves that once belonged to my grandmother, and its row of deep red spines stands out starkly against the mixed colors of faded dust covers and trade paper-backs there. Throughout my childhood, both before and after my grandmother's death, I respectfully approached those shelves each time I visited her house. The Harvard Classics—the idea of them as well as their physical presence—came to fascinate me, in part I suppose for the reason that such projects appeal to so many: they suggest the existence of a fixed canon that might in time be conquered. For this reason and a host of others not im-mediately relevant, I decided to read the Classics, in their entirety, over the course of a year, and to write something about the ex-perience, about what it felt like to immerse myself in them.

When I first told people—both friends and publishing profes-sionals—about my plan, I tended to focus on the eccentricity of the project, to play up the difficulty of reading all of "the Classics" in a single year. This seemed like a natural point of emphasis, in part because of a recent explosion of books about intrepid experi-mentalists who have given over a year of their lives to single-minded and unlikely pursuits—obeying all of the Mosaic laws, say, or fol-lowing every recipe in Julia Child's *Mastering the Art of French Cook-ing*—a genre that I have heard called "stunt books," but which I came to term, while working on my own contribution to the field, A-Year-of-Riding-the-Unicycle Memoirs.

When I proposed to read the Five Foot Shelf, I meant to piggy-back shamelessly on the success of these AYORTUMers. (There is even a subgenre dedicated to reading multivolume sets like the *En-cyclopedia Britannica* and *Oxford English Dictionary*, which offered pre-cedents for my project.) Thus, I framed the book I planned to write in terms of the oddity of my undertaking. But before long I came to understand that my book wasn't a great candidate for the genre, above all because, *qua* single-minded and unlikely pursuit, there wasn't much to it. Even though the year proved difficult in many ways (about which difficulties, more below), there was never any drama as to whether I would read all the books "on time." Finishing the Shelf in a year meant reading roughly 450 pages a week, which is probably about an average page count for the serious amateur reader. For the professional—book critic, academic, acquiring editor at a publishing house—it's junior varsity stuff.

Besides which, the Shelf isn't a reference set. These weren't dictionary or encyclopedia pages but pages written to be read in much the way I proposed to read them. This distinction points to the deeper reason that my book would not have made much of an AYORTUMer. As I've said, the Classics were meant to represent—really, to contain—a "liberal education," to make such an education available to the autodidactic everyman. But by the time I started reading them, I had already ostensibly completed my liberal education when I graduated from college (albeit, not from Harvard) with a degree in English. I'd guess that the typical AYORTUM-reader also has a liberal education, if we define such a thing roughly as an undergraduate degree in the humanities. And so the unicycle memoir I had considered would have amounted to a book by and for the liberally educated about the "stunt" of attempting to acquire a liberal education. It's probably fairly obvious that such a book—more bicycle than unicycle—wouldn't work very well.

On the plus side, the idea points the way toward another, less stunty kind of book, one that also has a number of precedents, in which the liberally educated author returns to said education in order to remind himself, and his l-e'ed readers, of the value of said l.e. Thus, a film critic from the *New Yorker* enrolls in Columbia's humanities track, or a retiring academic heads to St. John's College to follow its "Great Books" curriculum. The problem here is that, when it came down to it, there was surprisingly little overlap between the actual Harvard Classics and the liberal education that I, for one, received. This is so, in part, because there is no longer such a thing as *a* liberal education, one that all liberally educated people share in common. And here we might circle back a bit to note that the single greatest reason that such a shared liberal education no longer exists can be located in the person of Charles Eliot.

I didn't understand this last point until after I started doing research for my book and learned Eliot's story. Even then, I didn't pursue the line of thought too far, because I was busy reading through the Shelf. At most, it struck me as a curious irony that Eliot's name should be remembered by way of the Classics, given his real influence.

But once my reading project was done, it came time to write the book, and I thought more about Eliot's legacy. The connection between Eliot and the first "great books" set no longer seemed ironic. It seemed quite natural, in fact, provided one understood the meaning of Classics a bit differently. It's one thing for a champion of "liberal education" to speak of fitting such a thing within a five foot shelf; it's quite another for a founder of the research university to do so. In the latter case, the existence—and the success—of the Classics might be seen not as a blow against specialization, but as its final victory. If a classical education can be fit on a shelf, sold door-to-door, placed in every home, then Eliot's modern university can happily dispose of it and get about its proper business. When I think now about the Five Foot Shelf, I am reminded of the colloquial meaning of "putting something on the shelf." A great-books set, while not quite a means of shelving the classics, allows us at least to table them for a while. By comparing my decision to read these books to conquering the entire *Encyclopedia Britannica*—by suggesting that taking the classics down from the shelf was an act of eccentricity—I was unwittingly supporting this end. But this isn't the spirit in which I read. It didn't feel, when I did it, like a stunt; it felt like life.

4

I was left, then, with a book about reading. Of course, there are lots of these, too. David Foster Wallace once noted that characters on television spend almost no time watching TV, despite the fact that most Americans spend an inordinate number of hours doing so. To Wallace, this suggested a particularly vicious feedback loop between watcher and watched. But he also acknowledged that a television show in which people sit around for hours at a time watching television would be less than thrilling. Though there are a great many books that are ostensibly about reading, a book about someone sitting on a couch somewhere, slowly turning pages, wouldn't be especially tantalizing, either. And so writing about the year I spent reading the Classics meant writing, by and large, about what happened when the books went back up on the shelf.

Here we come to the year's above-mentioned difficulties. Of these there were many—it was the most difficult year of my life, in fact—but all the others paled beside one: a person I love as much as I love anyone in the world got sick, and suffered, and died. This is the one universal experience that has survived the balkanization of education and culture: the people we love most—including ourselves—will all eventually die. Proponents of "liberal education" must reckon with the fact that scientific specialization allows us to live, on balance, longer than we used to, and that the lives we live tend to be more materially comfortable than they once were. But proponents of specialization must admit that the stay of execution that science offers can only ever be temporary and that, for all the questions that science has answered for us, it can't tell us what it means that we must all die. It can't tell us what compensation we might find for the brevity of our lives, or what consolation we might find for the brevity of the lives of others.

The book I wound up writing, then, is in large part about the search for this compensation and consolation. It won't surprise you to hear that I found these two things—to the extent that I found them at all—in the books that I read that year. Perhaps if I'd been riding the unicycle, or reading the *OED*, I would have found consolation in these pursuits. But the more I read, the clearer it became that confronting the problem of death—a problem that will never go away—is the reason the classics exist, while such things as unicycles and dictionaries and French cooking exist for very different reasons, however pressing those reasons may be. For this reason, what began as a stunt became a necessity.

"Every reader finds himself," Proust once wrote about the true nature of great literature. "The writer's work is merely a kind of optical instrument that makes it possible for the reader to discern what, without this book, he would perhaps never have seen in himself." This seems just right to me. Finally, it's not that I found consolation from the classics, but that I found consolation in the world by reading the classics. I found consolation in living a life that included these books. And so the book I finally did write wasn't a book about reading so much as a book about the life of one reader. It was a book about the instruments that made it possible for me to read myself.